MW00653498

BEYOND *Good Intentions*

The Art of Christian Living

JUAN LUIS LORDA

From the original Spanish *Moral: El Arte de Vivir* © 2006 Ediciones Palabra, S.A., Madrid, Spain, © 1993 Juan Luis Lorda. Translated by Raul Alessandri and Bernard Browne and reprinted with permission.

Scripture texts from the New and Old Testaments are taken from The Holy Bible Revised Standard Catholic Edition © 1965 and 1966 by the Division of Christian Education of the National Council of the Churches of Christ in the United States. All rights reserved. All copyrighted material is used by permission of the copyright owner. No part of it may be reproduced without permission in writing from the copyright owner.

Copyright © 2013, Scepter Publishers, Inc. The total or partial reproduction of this book is not permitted, nor its informatic treatment, or the transmission of any form or by any means, either electronic, mechanic, photocopy, or other methods, without the prior written permission of the owners of the copyright.

Scepter Publishers, Inc.
PO Box 1391
New Rochelle, NY 10802
www.scepterpublishers.org

Composition, cover and text design by Rose Design

Printed in the United States of America

ISBN: 978-1-59417-183-3

CONTENTS

PART II: RESPECT

PART III: GRACE

FOREWORD

Every book has its own story, and every reader has a right to know something about it.

This book had its origin when Professor Luis de Moya suffered a terrible accident that made it impossible to continue teaching his course on moral theology and I had to step in for him. I prepared a brief course presenting Christian morals as best I could. I had some prior ideas. I wanted to show that morality is linked to our natural human feelings and can lead us to fulfillment. So I taught the classes, answered questions, made notes of students' criticisms and suggestions.

Then I thought of writing a book. It seemed to me that this would be the right time, considering how many books on ethics are already available that try to offer a substitute for Christian morality, with greater or less success.

I once read an interview with film director George Lucas in which he said he tried to make movies he'd like to see. In writing this book, I've adopted the same good idea. I like books that are brief, profound, well organized and easy to read. A book on morals needs to show the reasonableness and beauty of Christian living and encourage readers to improve. That's what I have tried to do. I have done a lot of rewriting, for a book is a work of art, not just a bowl of ideas but more like a painted landscape in which each stroke requires consideration (to be in the right place) and must be corrected many times.

Within the limitations of its few pages and simple approach, this little volume does not confine itself to repeating well-known ideas. If it has any value, that's because it presents ideas in circulation among people who've tried to present a positive and responsible approach to morality. Christian reflection of this sort has been particularly rich in recent years, culminating in the encyclical *Veritatis Splendor* of John Paul II. (At the conclusion, I list some of the sources I've used.)

So that is this book's history, and why I chose to dedicate it to Luis de Moya.

Juan Luis Lorda
Pamplona, Spain, 2006

PART I

TRUTH

The five chapters of this first part explain (1) what morality is, and how the moral sense arises and develops as a person reaches maturity; and (2) the goods and duties that provide the basis for human choices. This leads to (3) the role of conscience, including values and the order of priority among them; (4) human weakness, including the strange and mysterious conflict between what one is and what one ought to be; and finally (5) freedom, the framework in which morality exists and is realized.

Part I is titled "Truth" because all the elements considered lead to knowledge of the truth and the possibility of acting according to it—"walking in the truth," as St. Teresa might have said, or "living in the truth," as Vaclav Havel or Pope John Paul II would put it. The moral life as a whole consists of the effort to live in accordance with the truth of things and of man.

1

What Morality Is and Is Not

What Morality Is Not

We need to begin with *what morality is not* in order to explain later *what morality is.* Unless the prejudices and misunderstandings are removed, we can't move forward.

People speak of morality all the time: in the family, with friends, at work, in the media, in government. Everyone is interested because everyone is affected, and everyone has something to say. That makes it both difficult and easy to talk about morality. Easy because everyone has an opinion—which in turn makes it hard to get others to listen and agree. About no other topic do people argue so much. The clashing opinions rule out compromise. This lends support to the notion that right and wrong exist in the realm of personal opinion, where each individual can and should think as he likes and no particular opinion can be imposed. The only consensus, it seems, is that nothing is certain here.

In scientific and technical fields that deal with objective matters, sure knowledge is possible and there are few opinions: one either knows or does not know a matter of fact. He or she who knows the facts gets to say what they are. But in art and in morality it's apparently different: instead of facts, we're dealing with feelings and preferences, interests or points of view. Everything is subjective, a matter of opinion.

Morality also seems to vary with peoples, cultures, and eras. This makes it seem even more unstable and provisional. People today have the sense of living in a new epoch that has moved beyond the morality of ages past. Traditional morality in the West, which used to have a Christian foundation, seems to have been superseded. The image of it that remains is quite negative and strange, though somewhat vague inasmuch as people don't really know what it was. Traditional morality for too many consists of a set of norms—fixed, strict commandments, especially in sexual matters—that people learned while growing up and that kept them more or less repressed all their lives, worrying about whether they would end up in heaven or hell.

Christian morality, according to this thinking, could be compared to a pinball game. Life begins when the metal ball starts its run, and it proceeds as the ball meanders here or there, gaining or losing points. At the end, the points are added up, and if you have enough points, you win a prize. Otherwise you lose. And so also with Christian morality: total up the sins and good actions, then go to heaven or to hell.

By this standard, we've made considerable progress. Society has sloughed off excessive restrictions and achieved a much freer and open mentality. Progress apparently has come from getting rid of those external, arbitrary norms designed and imposed by narrow-minded people in order to keep everybody under control. As the old joke said, "everything that's good is either fattening or a sin." Morality like that seems to be a thing of the past. Prohibitions and repressions have disappeared, and the world keeps going around just as it always has.

With that mountain of precepts overcome, the only moral principle remaining for most people is good intentions. A good person has good intentions, and that's enough. Then you can act and think however you want, provided you let your neighbor do the same.

What a person wants to do with his life is thus a private matter, and nobody else can enter someone else's private life without authorization. No one can set himself up as judge of his neighbor's morals or place restrictions on the other fellow beyond those arising from the clash of individual rights, where it's the job of government to adjudicate. (But the minimum regulation required for peaceful coexistence is best, with good intentions otherwise sufficient.)

True, some things at first seem wrong to everyone. Most people think it's wrong to kill a child or hit an old person without reason or abuse an animal or pollute a river. But explaining why these things are wrong is not so easy. Very likely, the best we could do would be to agree that they *look* bad. Or someone seeking a utilitarian reason might say such things are bad because coexistence would suffer if the behavior became widespread. Social life would be difficult if anyone and everyone could claim a right to punch us if he felt like it. So there are laws against doing that.

Here the operative principle is practicality. But not in other cases. For example: animal abuse. Why can't I hit my dog, if I don't bother anyone else in doing it? You might say somebody who abuses animals may feel tempted to abuse people. But the argument isn't very solid, and it lends itself to endless casuistry: "What if it's just a little . . . ?"

In the end, the most we could say is that morality consists of a set of norms agreed upon to make coexistence possible. During the last two centuries, ethical investigation hasn't gotten much further than that, aside from putting it in a more elegant, complex, and comprehensive way.

What Morality Is

In reality, morality has little or nothing to do with opinions, normative systems, good intentions, or coexistence. A simple definition of morality is that it's the *art of living*. That is all.

Let's look at the terms of this definition. Morality is an art, as are painting, writing, knowing how to sell things, playing the piano, or carving wood. Art is understood as a set of theoretical and technical abilities that combine the experience and dexterity needed to do something well.

Knowledge of a theoretical and technical nature, experience, dexterity—these elements are necessary for an art. To play the piano, for example, requires theoretical knowledge of music, techniques regarding the moving of one's fingers, etc. Adeptness in putting the theoretical knowledge to work is then acquired through exercise (practice in moving one's fingers, reading music, etc.). Becoming a master requires mastery of both the theoretical and practical. It doesn't help to know how to play a piano without ever putting one's hands to the keys, nor is dexterity enough if you can't read music.

Morality, too, is an art—the art of living well. What does that mean? The answer is simple: To live well means to live in a way proper to a human being. As the art of painting is to paint, so *morality is the art of living as a human being.*

This may seem surprising. We're already persons, so why not just live naturally, let ourselves go? But although that's all it takes to be alive, it isn't enough to live in a way fit for a human being. It may work for animals, but not for us.

A human being is something special, a free being. Among other things, freedom means being far less conditioned than animals by instincts; but for the same reason, we need to learn many things animals know instinctively, as well as many others entirely unknown to animals that are proper to human beings. Men and women need to be educated to live like human beings. If they aren't educated, they live like poorly prepared animals. Indeed, without education people are not likely to survive. An infant is naturally vulnerable, able to do hardly anything by himself. In the first months, everything must be done for him, and afterward he must be taught even the most elementary things.

The young child also needs to learn what is proper to human beings: how to talk, write, behave toward others, and a thousand other things. Unless he is educated, he does not develop those capacities. If isolated from talking people, he does not learn to talk; if his environment is not stimulating, he does not develop cultural capacities like artistic or musical sensibility or even gastronomical refinement. A person comes into the world with natural capacities, but developing them requires education.

Freedom is the most important and most characteristic of our human capacities. It is the one that needs to be educated with the greatest care. To educate a person means, above all, teaching him or her to use freedom properly, in a way proper to a human person.

Children lack instinctive knowledge of how to use their freedom. They have some natural inclination to use it well, just as they also have a natural inclination to talk and to walk, but they need education. Little by little they must learn what a person ought to do and ought to avoid, what is suitable and unsuitable.

Now we can better understand what morality is. It is *the art of using one's freedom well.* This is an art we all must learn to live properly.

It's an art because it requires theoretical and practical knowledge that must be received from others, along with habits acquired by practice. First, knowledge: we have to learn from other human beings how a human being ought to behave. Then habits: because it's not enough to know how to behave—one must be in the habit of behaving properly.

If people were only minds, it would be enough to think of something and make up one's mind to do it. But we know from experience that there are many things we'd like to do but don't do. Something gets in the way. Carrying out a decision requires *willpower*, and when that fails, we may not do what we decide.

Willpower varies from person to person. It has a lot to do with each one's customs or habits. For example, getting up as soon as the alarm rings requires that one be accustomed to doing that. Just wishing is usually not enough. True, everyone gets up promptly in exceptional circumstances. But in ordinary circumstances people without that habit will often fail.

Someone who starts work promptly has that good habit, and work becomes easier. Someone used to delaying when he doesn't feel like working has a bad habit that makes work more difficult. Over many years, there's a huge difference between having and not having this good habit. It's a matter of thousands and thousands of working hours and the productiveness of a life.

Habits make or destroy a person. They reinforce freedom or reduce it. They supply the necessary link between what a person wants to do and what he can do. They are sources of the knowledge and freedom needed to function as a human being. The very word morality comes from the Latin word *mos*, meaning *custom or habit.* It's an old meaning, always valid: *morality is the art of good habits*—that is to say, of habits that are good for the person, suit him, give him maturity and perfection.

We have proposed three definitions of morality up to now: the art of living well, living in the way proper to a human being; education in the use of freedom; and, finally, acquiring good habits. Thus, morality consists in knowing, practicing, and developing good customs that enables one to live in a manner proper to a human being.

Morality as Art

Morality is certainly an art. But lacking a theoretical basis, it's impossible to give proper direction to one's practice of an art. And without practice, it's impossible to do things well. Just as nobody plays the piano simply by wanting to play it well, so just wanting to be good and not harming anybody is not enough. Throughout history, many barbaric deeds have been done without evil intentions and even in the belief that they rendered a great service to humanity. Good intentions are only a first step.

But training in an art must be done properly. Every beginner puts his fingers on the wrong piano keys once in a while. But if a beginner gets used to making mistakes, he will develop vices difficult or impossible to overcome, and will remain a mediocre pianist. A master can't allow himself even minute errors. Every mistake is a step back.

This is a universal law of human action. Each conscious action by a person leaves a trace, more or less strong according to the action's intensity and its repetition. Mistakes leave marks that by repetition can become bad habits, whereas by repetition right actions can become good habits. Habits are created and destroyed in this way in all fields, including sports, physical abilities and skills, the arts, and morality.

Strange to say, some people believe this in regard to everything except what pertains to morality. They imagine that morality is entirely arbitrary, a matter of opinion, not bound by natural laws. But that is a mistake. Living worthily as a human person requires effort and training. It's an art whose practice improves when done well and deteriorates when done poorly. Good habits are in play in each free decision. The accumulation of good or bad decisions and the intensity of those decisions leave a trail of habits that make a person either more mature and free or less so.

The art of good living is no more a matter of opinion than is the art of piano playing.

At the same time, of course, human action is also strongly conditioned by prior realities. We haven't made ourselves. Almost everything we are was *present* when we came into the world. Long before we could use our freedom, we were formed and conditioned by our human nature. Only to some extent can we change ourselves: our creativity has limited room for operation.

There is a part of us which is the product of our free decisions, but the greater part is not: we have received it and it has its laws. We can't decide how we will digest food or in what direction our blood will flow. The body operates by laws we have not invented and can barely modify (generally, the most we can do is discover them). And what is true in the physical sphere parallels what is true in the spiritual sphere, the setting where freedom operates.

Most of the moral life consists of freely developing capacities we already possessed when we came into the world. These capacities have their laws, although we may not know them. Intelligence, for example, has its own way of intuiting and reasoning, ways we haven't invented. The will, like other capacities, also has its laws, which are not for us to invent. We can't invent freedom, love, friendship, happiness.

So morality doesn't depend on our personal preferences. It's not a matter of opinion, except in the limited sense that, not knowing what's right in a particular situation, our opinions may come into play.

It's the same with medicine. Doctors also give opinions when they aren't sure, but they know their opinions don't change reality. One might express the opinion that some food is or isn't poisonous, but the opinion doesn't alter the fact: the food is either poisonous or it isn't.

Moral knowledge is difficult to attain. It requires an effort, but the effort is worth it, since this is precious knowledge. Moreover, there are ways of becoming oriented to what's good and what's bad. Let's briefly consider what that means.

Nature responds well to what's good and badly to what isn't. This is so in all fields, though not in the same way. If you eat something that isn't good for you, physical signs soon tell you of your mistake. People around you may become aware of it too. Physical mistakes and good choices have physical manifestations.

Morality is a little different. Errors and good choices in the use of freedom can't be felt physically. Yet they are somehow perceptible. Thus we say we *feel good* when we act well and *feel badly* when we act badly. These feelings are not precise indicators, but they do give hints. Acting well leaves a sense of happiness; dissatisfaction and displeasure follow a wrong choice.

There is another important external criterion. Good actions are perceived as beautiful and desirable. When they are very good, they evoke admiration and the desire to imitate them. They give pleasure to the one who sees them, similar to the pleasure of looking at a beautiful landscape. Everyone recognizes the beauty of the action of a person who risks his life to save another. Any normal person would like to be like that, although he may not feel capable of it. Contemplating a very good or heroic action, we feel approval, intuit that something worthy of humanity has happened, and have a sense of pleasure that a human being could do something so noble.

Bad actions, on the other hand, are perceived as ignoble, improper, and ugly. They prompt spontaneous rejection. No one needs persuading that it's bad to make an animal suffer or, even more, a human being. It would have been better not to have seen the deed, better that it not have happened.

A bad action is aesthetically off-key. We tell small children that something bad is ugly. We educate them morally by teaching them to feel repugnance for what is bad.

But people can lose their good taste. They can even reach the point of considering beautiful, or at least desirable, what everybody else naturally deems ugly and hateful. Some people enjoy torturing rabbits, others enjoy torturing people. This doesn't make these actions matters of opinion or mean that a sadist's tastes are just as good as anyone else's. It simply means that the natural moral sense—moral good taste—can become distorted. But in the end everyone knows that a person who enjoys making others suffer is correctly labeled a psychopath, a degenerate—not just for utilitarian reasons (a habit like that could have unpleasant consequences for society), but because of the spontaneously perceived ugliness of the action grounded in a natural sense of what is suitable or unsuitable for a person.

The aesthetic character of human action is very important in moral education. To some extent, we could say morality is simply the aesthetics of the spirit, good taste in regard to human behavior.

Aristotle said that to educate a person was to teach him good taste in reference to his behavior: to lead him to love the beautiful and abhor the ugly. It means guiding and reinforcing the natural reactions to noble and ignoble actions. Believing beauty to be the fundamental tool by which to teach morals, the Greeks wanted their children to admire and imitate the heroic deeds of their traditions as expressed in literature and history. In fact, they thought the purpose of literature and history to be the moral education of the young.

Plainly this supposes a very high idea of a person. It also implies a worthy way of living, along with the view that education aims to help a child to love that way of life, and develop habits by which he can behave like that.

At times our culture calls all that into question. Uncertain whether there is a moral way of living worthy of a human being, it doesn't know how to educate. It can instruct and inform a child about many things (the orbit of the planets, the function of chlorophyll, the French Revolution), but it doesn't know how to tell the child what to do with his or her life.

Even so, human beings haven't ceased being human and the language of beauty developed by the Greeks remains valid. There still are beautiful, noble actions, and ugly, ignoble ones. The former confirm the reality of human dignity. And as a matter of fact so do the others, for to call something ignoble and unworthy of a person, one must have an idea of what is noble and worthy.

This points to a conclusion: if there is a way of living worthy of a human being, it's worth doing everything possible to find it. Difficult as that may be, it would be sad to let life run its course without discovering what is most important.

Christian Morality

How do we know what's worthy of a person? How can we learn to live as a human being should? The first step, no doubt, is to develop an inclination toward beautiful actions—an admiration for what is beautiful and a desire to imitate it. The first step toward having a moral sense is to desire a life full of beauty.

But this has limitations. The natural sense of what is good and what is bad—moral aestheticism—offers clear guidance in extreme cases, but it doesn't cover the whole field of human behavior. If a situation is complicated or many factors are involved, doubts may arise. There's nothing surprising in that—it's the same in other areas of human experience. Appearance or smell makes some foods instinctively attractive and others instinctively repugnant; but often look and smell don't tell us anything and may even deceive us.

We know what is edible and what is noxious largely from the experience of those who've passed what they learned on to us. Culture preserves and transmits the experience of those who go before us. It's a medium for knowledge we wouldn't have acquired on our own. Suppose each human being had to discover everything from scratch: one mistake—one poisonous mushroom—could send you to the grave. The experience accumulated and transmitted by culture preserves people from that fate.

There is also a great deal of transmitted experience in the moral area. Those who preceded us accumulated knowledge about what is and isn't proper for a person. This knowledge is more subtle than with mushrooms, since what pertains to human freedom is much richer and more complex than what pertains to food.

But doubts can creep in at times, and the experience of different cultures may differ. Working only on the surface, one would make mistakes by simplistic comparisons of the moral norms of different cultures. One needs to go very deeply into a culture to comprehend the moral meaning of how people behave. Each must be considered in its context: a culture possesses a logic that can be appreciated only if we know it well. That is why the notion of developing a common morality or of reaching something like a common denominator of all moralities turns out to be artificial and impossible in practice.

What nevertheless is truly important about the different moral experiences of humanity is that there is a common moral concern, and all peoples have understood that the most important part of education lies in transmitting it—that is, teaching the young how to live properly.

It's hardly a secret that our culture is perplexed: it doesn't know what to transmit to the young. Indeed, at the moment it seems unsure of what it means to be human. We have lost a good deal of our patrimony.

This may be why culture today appears to be attempting to assimilate proposals from diverse moral sources, albeit in bits and pieces. The result is like trying to do a puzzle with many missing pieces. Given all the different sources, there's no telling what to choose.

To be able to choose among all these moral systems, you would have to experience each of them, and determine whether and to what extent it can make human life something worth living. But that's impossible, since ultimately a really adequate test of each would require living an entire life that way. Nor is it possible to make a kind of synthesis of moralities. Each has its own genius and resists being mixed with others.

In offering Christian morality here, we offer a morality that's already been tested. This is the morality that led to the development of the West and that it still professes. This also is the most universal morality, since it has reached all parts of the world: peoples of all cultures have lived according to it and still do. Thus it is the most important morality that has ever existed. Obviously that doesn't show that it's true, but it constitutes a reasonable basis for someone to learn it well since no other moral system in history has had such immense and deep cultural impact.

Still, the validity of a morality can't be demonstrated like a mathematical theorem. Certainty regarding the truth of morality arises from its good results for the person, its beauty and its outcome, not only personal but social. That's how it is with Christian morality.

But we need to recognize that Christian morality is unusual in that *it is a revealed morality.* It does not claim to be simply the result of accumulated human experiences, but the teaching of God. Christians believe that God, the creator of everything, revealed to humans the way of living suitable for them.

You might say this morality is something like the manufacturer's instructions that come with products. The manufacturer explains the best way to use the product. And we're glad, because then we can treat the product properly and it lasts longer and works better. Of course, some people are too impatient to read the instructions or look at them only after they've damaged the product. But such behavior isn't reasonable. With instructions at hand, it's reasonable to read them.

Christian morality represents the instructions of the manufacturer. Those instructions perfect and complete the knowledge we can acquire from experience and studying the product, in this case, the person. It includes what is fundamental to all moralities, drawing upon the knowledge that lies deep in the human heart.

The most serious objection raised to Christian morality is that it comes from ages past. C.S. Lewis calls this the "chronological prejudice"—the idea that whatever is older must have been surpassed. It's like thinking sunsets have been surpassed because they've been around for billions of years.

There are many offerings in the moral marketplace today but no substitute for the real thing. We should not be deceived by some competing product's wrapping. No other moral system has such high quality or offers such guarantees as Christian morality does. It has illuminated the lives of millions and bestowed on humanity the benefits of heroism, authenticity, and beauty. It would be madness to pass by without trying it.

2

The Voice of Nature

A Non-centered Being

The last chapter developed the idea that morality is the art of living as a human being. We've seen the importance of freedom in doing this. Human beings are, properly, free. This is the clearest difference between them and the animals. The bodily differences aren't so great—favorable to humans in some respects, to animals in others, and in general not very important. But what really distinguishes man is freedom.

The human person owns himself. He does what he wants, moves after mental deliberation, is master of his actions, is not governed by instincts. Yes, instincts sometimes can carry us away and dominate us (as in a perilous situation). But ordinarily intellect governs, and we decide freely what to do. By contrast, animals act as instinct tells them. Each stimulus evokes its response, according to complex patterns yet to a great extent fixed and, in general, guaranteeing the survival of the individual and the species (attack, defend, flee, feed, reproduce).

Instincts control the whole life of animals. They are interested in the environment only for their needs. Otherwise they don't even notice it. Except that it's natural to them, we could say animals are profoundly selfish: they live for themselves.

When a need arises, the instinct leads the animal to satisfy it. As soon as he feels hungry, for instance, a window to his surroundings opens up, oriented to its objective: to eat. He looks for food and has no interest in anything else.

A hungry lion looking at a gazelle sees it only as food, and ignores its beautiful colors and the elegance of its movements. It's said that dogs pulling the sled of a scientific expedition in Siberia, rushed to eat the meat of a newly discovered frozen mammoth, ignoring the scientific importance of the find. Here was meat, that's all.

Human beings can escape the closed world of instincts precisely because they have intelligence. Until intelligence develops, small children act very much like the animals, controlled by instincts and relating to the environment only to satisfy their needs. They are terribly selfish, act only for themselves, seek only their own advantage. Don't expect a baby to be pleased at seeing another baby sharing his bottle. If he notices and is hungry, he won't tolerate it. Young children are not altruistic. That isn't their nature.

As intelligence develops, however, a child leaves that selfish universe. His relationship to the environment changes; not only does he know what interests him directly (food, drink, etc.), he discovers the things that are there, independently of his convenience. He is still very selfish, as he must be to survive, but he begins to discover the world beyond his needs and desires.

This is to say that the development of intelligence initiates an

objective relationship with things. The child discovers that other things have their own laws and needs. This is a fundamental step in the intellectual and moral life. Animals and small children operate as if they were the only ones in the world. But as intelligence develops, the child comes to realize that he is not the only center of reality, there are many others besides him. Now he can know things as things—know where they are, what they are like, where they come from. He can appreciate their appearance, color, smell, texture, even if they don't serve him. He can know truth and contemplate beauty. This makes him what philosopher and sociologist Helmuth Plessner calls a "non-centered being" who can take the point of view of things.

One might call this an *authentic conversion,* intellectual and moral. As the intellect opens up to the world and knows it as it is, one is in position to overcome one's instinctive selfishness. This is fundamental to understanding the way of living proper to humans—i.e., what morality is.

Goods and Duties

As people mature, coming to realize they aren't the only beings on earth and there are others with their own needs and demands, they find themselves confronting two different callings of nature: one coming mainly from the inside, the other from outside.

The first is the call from one's own being. Human beings have permanent needs like food and drink and can't stop seeing the environment in relation to those needs.

The second is the call from the things around one. Identifying with them in a way, we grasp that other beings also have needs and, by the same token, rights. Evidently there is more to life than simply pursuing what one needs or wants for oneself. Other things impose duties on oneself.

The first call is that of goods, the things that we need and that attract us. The second is the call of duties, the demands imposed by beings and realities around us. Let's look briefly at both.

A) *The call of goods*. Many centuries ago, Aristotle defined as goods those things that are desirable for a human being—things to which one feels inclined and which one longs for.

A healthy person, like all healthy animals, desires spontaneously what is advantageous: food, drink, etc. In principle, he desires goods, though in some cases he can err in the interpretation of what is good or how much he desires it. Those impulses are reinforced by the satisfaction produced by attaining goods (pleasure) or the harm of being deprived of them (pain). Experiences of pleasure and pain shape and educate instinctive behavior. Thus animals can be trained by a system of rewards and punishments.

As intelligence develops, the possibility of discovering goods expands enormously. Instincts seek goods conducive to survival, but intelligence goes much further. We learn quickly to desire as goods things useful to attain the primary goods: e.g., money, which isn't edible but can provide food and which to that extent is good. To discover it as a good, we need at least elementary reason. Animals can't grasps the relationship between money and food and therefore don't desire money. But children understand the relationship very easily and soon begin desiring money as a good, even though it can't be eaten. This relationship can't be discovered by instinct but only by the intellect.

Thus we learn to desire as goods other things useful to get or preserve comfort, security, or health. Since intelligence allows us to foresee the future, we discover as goods not only those that satisfy current needs but those that may come in handy in the future: e.g., one quickly learns that though one isn't hungry at this moment, it's good to store food or money.

When the child matures, he discovers that the field of goods extends far beyond primary needs and he becomes interested in numerous other goods. As his education dictates, he learns to appreciate goods related to personal realization: abilities, skills, knowledge; status, good name, professional success; relationships of friendship and love; aesthetic goods; and moral habits—virtues—that make a person truthful and honest. All these are goods precisely because they are desirable, and they are desired because they benefit us in one way or another.

In some cases, desire originates in our instinctive heritage, as with primary goods like food, drink, etc. In others, desire is generated by the intellect, which has discovered their usefulness (e.g., money). In still other cases, desire arises from some social circumstance leading us to consider and love them (social position, professional success, fame, etc.). The desire for aesthetic, religious, and moral goods requires a careful schooling that teaches us their beauty: one desires these goods only insofar as one has discovered their value.

The valuing of primary goods is automatic: we feel instinctively that they are good. The valuing of other goods is a result of intellect and education. First getting to *know* that they are good, we come to *feel* their goodness as we become attached to them. Then we love them with our whole being, not only our will, and are sad when they are missing and joyful when we have them. The child or adult who has learned that money is a good ends up feeling it as a good; he feels the money's attraction, and may indeed feel it as strongly as he feels hunger or thirst. So too with fame, status, work, sports, and all the other things to which we become attached. Once we feel them as goods, we are drawn to them.

Coming to appreciate as goods those that are real goods—that is, those that are truly worthwhile—is the most important part of education. It isn't easy. Someone who hasn't been taught to love *all* goods may become dominated by the primary goods—food, drink, comfort, sex, security, health, etc.—or by other acquired attachments (money, gambling, etc.).

Obviously important as they are, the primary goods can't be despised. But it's unworthy of a human being to devote his or her whole life to them since a person is capable of much more. *Primum vivere deinde philosophare,* said the classic adage: "First one has to live, then one can philosophize." Quite true: we can't live as if we didn't have to eat, but neither should we live as if eating were all we had to do. The goods proper to being fully human must be set in order and sought.

Learning which are the goods of the human being and getting to love them is an important part of morality, but only part. Morality requires that, besides goods, we take account of duties.

B) *The call of duties* is the other voice of nature. It is the call of the things around us.

What we know first and best in the whole world is ourselves. Then we are led by experience to understand other things, reasoning that what is good for us must be good for the others and what is bad for us must be bad for them.

Animals, lacking intelligence, listen only to the voice of instinct. Humans listen also to the voices of the beings around us, and it is proper to humans to feel obligated by those voices. We can heed them precisely because we are endowed with intelligence, which breaks down the wall of instinct. Reason also leads us to feel obligated to treat other beings with respect. They exist independently of our needs; they exist in themselves with needs of their own.

Humans furthermore feel obligated by the things around them, even though those things may not serve them at all. A normal person cannot be at ease with a hungry person close by. He may not feel like helping the hungry man or get any benefit from it, but he does feel obligated to share his food. It's the proper thing for a human being to do, and he would have to be an insensitive brute not to be aware of that.

Here, too, intellect plays a role. Through personal experience and education, the field of our duties expands enormously: we become more sensitive to our surroundings and see more clearly what is expected of us.

Some obligations are felt spontaneously. A wounded person's groans, an animal's howls—these things compel us to help. We discover many other duties as we gain experience, perceiving that the people around us need not just food, but a word of encouragement, a smile, some fellowship. Analyzing experience expands our sensitivity to duties and helps us grasp what is expected of us.

In sum, then: human behavior is conditioned by two voices of nature, that of goods and that of duties. *Goods attract us, duties oblige us.* The attraction of goods is felt, especially by sensibility. The obligation of duties, on the other hand, is perceived mainly through the intellect. Human conduct is conditioned by goods and duties whose relationship we need to understand since sometimes they limit each other. Morality, the art of living well, is also the art of combining goods and duties, assigning each thing its place, putting order in our loves.

From Selfishness to the Sense of Duty

An unavoidable selfishness is characteristic of infants while the emergence of a sense of duty comes with maturity. Then behavior is no longer dominated by desires, and the demands imposed by reality are acknowledged. It is a sign of immaturity, on the other hand, to retain one's infantile egoism and persist in behavior focused exclusively on seeking what's good for oneself. The egoism of a child is unavoidable and forgivable, but selfishness in an adult reveals an unhinged personality: the body has matured but not the spirit.

Infantile selfishness also errs. When a child takes more food than he can eat, we say "his eyes are bigger than his stomach." As the child acquires experience, he learns to determine how much food is enough (though even then it's not always easy to act on this). Instinct is rather imprecise and must be regulated by sound reason. Intelligence enables one to determine whether the good presented by instinct is really good (should be desired), and to what extent.

Maturity requires authentic intellectual and moral conversion. Behavior must make the transition from being ruled by impulses to being guided by reason. One must learn to regulate instinctive, selfish, self-centered tendencies (the world of likes and desires) in order to make room for reality (the world of duties). Maturity requires and supposes the capacity to think things over objectively: to think about our surroundings, to think of the others.

The behavior of someone who fails to reach that goal remains, for all practical purposes, beyond the reach of morality. Rather than being properly human, it's the behavior proper to animals. Although the persistence of infantile selfishness isn't chosen, selfishness comes to dominate the person who doesn't learn habitually to do as duty dictates.

Human beings are typically absorbed by whatever they are concentrating on at any particular time. Someone concentrating on his own needs and desires has no room for anything else. He can't hear the voice of things and perceive duties. One doesn't decide not to think of others but simply doesn't think of them, living as if they did not exist and concentrating on oneself.

Learning to listen to duties is the work of a lifetime. It may be the most important of all conversions: the one that turns us into moral beings. But selfishness isn't overcome without constant efforts to look objectively at the world, lest we fall prey to our own interests.

Helping others overcome their infantile egoism is an important part of moral education. Children must be taught to think of others and treat each person and thing with the respect that he, she, it, or they deserve. "The fundamental attitude of respect," says Dietrich von Hildebrand, "is the basis of all forms of moral behavior towards our neighbors and towards ourselves." We should stimulate the child's sensibility to appreciate the voice of duties, and teach him the beauty and dignity of conduct guided by the truth of things, conduct that overcomes egoism. Thus the child will love truth and take it as his standard, his norm.

Three Types of Duties

Everything around us imposes duties. To live well is, in the end, to know how to give each thing the treatment it deserves. Now let's consider these duties.

The beings around us can be situated on three levels: God, people (including society and culture), and nature, the physical world. Each imposes duties on us. Here we shall briefly define them by formulas of Christian morality, with a chapter devoted to each later.

A) The first being is God. As God is a very special being, so our duties towards him must be very special. If God exists—and Christians believe he does—he must occupy first place in our lives. This is tersely expressed in the first Commandment: "You shall love the Lord your God with all your heart, and with all your soul, and with all your strength, and with all your mind."

This simple, categorical formula repeats the word "all" four times: *all* our heart, *all* our soul, *all* our strength, *all* our mind. That is the only way to deal with the Supreme Being as he deserves.

A nonbeliever may find it excessive to place God above everything, and it really would be excessive to depend on another person or on some other reality in this way. But God deserves dependence like this and is the only one who does, the one on whom we *must* depend absolutely.

As man is a limited being, weak and mortal, but with an insatiable thirst for plenitude and the absolute, he cannot help depending on something. When he doesn't depend on God, he seeks substitutes. But to depend on something that is not God, as if it were God, is terrible. This is *idolatry.* It is idolatry to love oneself to the extent of being a prisoner of one's likes or ambition, idolatry to be enthralled with money, sex, drugs, or anything else. Nothing on earth deserves absolute devotion. No tyrant can claim it.

Since only God can be loved with total love, it may seem that there is no place for other loves. But that isn't so. Christians believe the world has come from God's hand and everything good in it is willed by God. If God wills something, however, we should desire it too. Thus, when we love things because they are good and deserve it, we also love God, their creator. Loving God, we are obliged to love all things insofar as they are good. That is precisely the order of reality, the order of our loves.

To love things well means loving them according to the order willed by God. To love things without God or instead of God would be to love them badly. The order of love is the order of reality. What is greatest commands the greatest love, and all other loves follow in order.

B) In the scale of being, after God come our fellow men. The love we owe to the people around us is perfectly expressed in the commandment summing up the rest of the Decalogue: "Love your neighbor as yourself."

Love of God has to be absolute because we depend upon him absolutely. But our love for men should be according to measure, albeit a very demanding one: We must love them as we love ourselves. This means wanting for others what we would like for ourselves, and wanting them to avoid what we want to avoid. It is reasonable to love others this way because they are beings of the same kind as ourselves. For God, everything; for men, whatever we want for ourselves.

But obviously we can't love everyone with the same intensity. There are billions of human beings, most of whom we don't know.

So we are given a criterion of order: love thy neighbor. In other words, love those closest to you because of kinship, friendship, camaraderie, and also physical proximity.

This is a realistic principle. To love others is in practice to love those near us, to the extent they are near. Even if being pleasant to people we see occasionally comes easier, that usually isn't real love. The test of whether we love our fellow men is whether we love those with whom we live. It's a delusion to imagine you love those far away if you mistreat those close at hand. But people who try to love those who are close can also come to love those far away, since they become accustomed—they educate themselves—to loving.

Love "for our fellow men" takes in the range of cultural and social realities, products of history and of life in community: moral and juridical persons, institutions, traditions, and customs. In general, the whole human cultural patrimony imposes duties upon us. We shall consider this later.

C) Third, after God and our fellow men are the things around us—all of them, whether natural or artificial. All have some dignity that we must respect, and all impose duties that, though not as serious as those imposed by other people, can be grave and urgent.

The relationship of human beings with the world is expressed in Christian tradition by saying that man is the steward of the world. He has received dominion over the material world to cultivate it, and satisfy his needs. But he is a steward, not an owner, and he will have to account for his stewardship of the world. He can use things but not mistreat or destroy them at will.

The right to private property, a right over things, is a limited right, according to Christian tradition. Things may be mine, but I cannot do with them whatever I want: first, because other persons may have needs—and, to that extent, rights—regarding them, and second, because things themselves have a dignity that

I must respect. Even though some good thing is mine, destroying it on a whim is immoral. It is also immoral to destroy plants for no reason or make animals suffer; even failing to appreciate the beauty of the material world has an element of immorality.

The second part of this book will consider all these duties. For now, it's enough to keep in mind that there are three kinds of external realities that impose duties upon us: God, fellow men, and nature—material things—in general.

3

The Order of Loves

Combining Goods and Duties

Human behavior is conditioned by goods and duties. Goods are things we desire because they seem useful to us or we find them instinctively attractive. Duties are obligations imposed upon us by things around us. Now we turn to the question of priorities: what to love first? St. Augustine called virtue "the order of love" (*City of God*, XV, 22).

Goods and duties aren't opposed but complementary: to attend to duties is good, and to attend to goods is a duty. Let's look at both.

A) *It is a duty to listen to the appeal of goods*, that is, to seek and obtain the goods we need. In principle, we are attracted by a good because it is good for us.

We have duties toward ourselves. We, too, are part of nature, and if we are to treat all things with respect, it's reasonable to do the same with ourselves. There is a legitimate and good self-love that leads us to seek goods we need. Otherwise, we could not live.

It would be wrong to imagine that everything we like is bad in itself or at least suspect. Nature is well made, and in general the things we desire are really good and fitting for us—and, to that extent, also a duty. Primary goods attract us because we need them. There's nothing wrong with feeling the attraction, but it would be wrong to allow ourselves to pursue them in a disordered manner. The sexual impulse signals a need of human nature, procreation, and is something good in itself, though as we shall see later, it also has an order.

Christian morality is respectful of nature: it is based on the conviction that God's creation is good and it is good to live according to the truth of created things. Puritanism has always existed and sometimes it has distorted Christian morality, yet Christian morality understands that even the appeal of good to self-interest is a good thing. Errors are possible, and a person needs education so as to recognize and love all goods, but the natural end of human inclinations is good. Morality is based on that.

In principle, there is a duty to be found in the call a good makes to us. Food is a good, but to eat food is also a duty. We must eat, must drink and rest, must grow and mature in all aspects, physical and intellectual, deepen our formation and our culture, our social and economic position. Inclination to goods helps us survive and become better.

Not everything we like is really a good, however, nor is what we like more necessarily better than what we like less and to be sought in preference to it. Moreover, it's easy to be mistaken about what is suitable or the extent to which something (e.g., food) is suitable. We need to use criteria of order and measure.

Something becomes a duty only after the intellect has passed judgment. Intellect determines the order among the goods we want: what, how much, to what extent. Desire is only a hint: for it to be followed, conscience must approve. Goods become duties after evaluation by conscience.

B) *To follow the calling of duties is a good*—indeed, it is very good and desirable for a human being and gives him dignity. But listening to the voice of duties requires much strength, part of which comes from the profound conviction that living this way is good and beautiful.

Duty acquires enormous strength in someone who learns to love it as a good. Entirely unlike the stoic (or Kantian) imperative to comply with duty, this is a case of passionately loving duty. Thus a man who passionately loves his wife and children fulfills his duties to them with an intensity and thoroughness unimaginable by one who learns about duty by reading a book. Theory cannot substitute for the power of a properly directed passion.

A human being is a bodily being with feelings. Those feelings are necessary for him to act forcefully, deeply, and perseveringly. A single decision may not suffice for the fulfillment of a difficult duty or one requiring a continued effort. But loving the duty does confer extraordinary strength for fulfillment. And then it is the whole person, body and soul, who loves.

A good mother is capable of incredible self-sacrifice for her children. Her feelings help her fulfill her obligations, even to a heroic degree. A professor with a vocation to teach or a craftsman who loves his work can draw extraordinary energy and spirit of sacrifice from the affection he feels toward his duties. Most remarkable of all, such people don't feel unhappy in sacrificing themselves but find pleasure in carrying the fulfillment of duty to an extreme. They love their duty with body and soul, and this profound affection reinforces the decision of their wills.

Feelings, however, are not easily controlled. Feelings also have a physical basis and are highly conditioned by factors beyond our control (climate, health, hunger, etc.). They are guided by intellect to a limited extent but slow to apprehend things as good. They must be educated and formed in the love of duty.

Often, in fact, we must fulfill duties without feeling any attraction or even while feeling repugnance. Forcing oneself to do what has to be done, with or without positive feelings, teaches our feelings and makes them more ready to follow the will's decision. Strong decisions carry the feelings with them; and their repetition creates habits.

Well-educated feelings sustain the moral life, giving it stability and consistency. A fundamental aspect of moral education thus lies in teaching children to love correct behavior and feel repugnance for disorderly conduct by showing the beauty of the former and the ugliness of the latter.

The eyes see and appreciate the good more quickly than the intellect does. Plato says a young person "will praise enthusiastically the beauty that he sees, will admit it into his soul, will feed on it, and in this way will acquire virtue," while "the ugly he would rightly disapprove of and hate while still young and unable to apprehend the reason, but when reason came the man thus nurtured would be the first to give her welcome, for by this affinity he would know her" (*Republic*. 402 A).

The Judgment of Conscience

Not even in an extreme situation may the father of a family or anyone else responsible for other people satisfy his own hunger without first attending to the hunger of those in his care. His hunger, no matter how real, is not his first priority.

Although hunger is a summons to satisfy a basic need, we needn't always heed its voice—we don't have to eat every time we feel hungry. Indeed, it may be better to eat at fixed times instead of responding to every twinge of hunger. Nor should we be guided only by taste and smell. A balanced diet is best and that requires a variety of foods, some tastier than others. Eating until you're stuffed is also a bad idea—better to leave the table when you could still eat a little more, lest you start putting on weight. Intelligence must control the voice of desire, determining when, how, and to what extent.

We are limited in our strength and the time at our disposal, with many goods to acquire and many duties to attend to. It's impossible to do everything at once. We need to establish order and measure in both the overall organization and allotment of our time and energy and also in our daily schedule.

Start with *measure*. Many goods are good only in proper measure: primary goods like comfort, health, food, and drink, as well as other potentially absorbing goods like money, prestige, work, and hobbies. In fact, all goods except the highest—love of God and love of neighbor—call for measure. Without measure, the resulting excess does us harm, either physically (food, alcohol) or because so much energy and time are expended that other things are neglected.

Next we need an *order of priorities*. Unable to do everything at once, we must choose what we'll do here and now. Goods and duties must be arranged in order. Sometimes there are conflicts: you can't work and rest at the same time, take care of a sick person and watch a movie, visit all your relatives simultaneously. So you must give thought to balancing different goods and duties.

Doing that comes more or less naturally. We consider possible courses of action and decide which goods to forgo, which duties to postpone. This evaluation, made almost without noticing it, is what is called "the voice of conscience." It amounts to this: *the natural capacity to be aware in each case of what I ought to do and, concretely, what duty or good I should attend to first*. Conscience determines priorities and, in the case of goods, questions of degree and extent.

What we shall do comes later: it is a decision to follow or not follow the judgment of conscience. Conscience and will are different. The role of conscience is to determine what is right by the use of intelligence.

Using the information at hand, we conclude that a particular way of acting is best because it best corresponds to the goods and duties in this particular case. We call this *the voice of conscience* because it is not something we create but something arising from the concrete situation.

This is the most proper and interior act of the person, in which intelligence and will interact. A life is judged in relation to these repeated moments, and a man is said to be honest who is guided by the voice of his conscience.

While the judgment of conscience comes before action, it is repeated after it. We evaluate the results to determine whether we have acted properly and followed the voice of conscience.

In acting contrary to conscience, one attacks the most delicate and intimate part of personhood, that which makes us free, and something breaks down inside us. That is why acting against conscience produces remorse. If, however, a person becomes accustomed to acting against conscience, conscience deteriorates—the light that makes us free is snuffed out. A person who doesn't respect his or her conscience ends by not knowing what is just and is prey to the irrational forces of instinct, inclination, and external pressure.

Conscience begins to function when intelligence does, and the two reach maturity together. Beginning to know the world, one begins to perceive duties and to start weighing how one should act. It's commonly supposed that the sense of responsibility emerges together with reason, around the age of seven.

Conscience is exquisitely *personal*. Although we can be helped, nobody else can decide for us. That's how it is with all the operations of intelligence: no one can understand for another. Here is what makes education so complex. A teacher is a facilitator, but the student is the one who must learn. No one can think for another or exercise freedom for another.

Imposing our opinions on others by force is wrong because it is contrary to the nature of freedom. Nor should anyone be forced to act against his conscience, since that would destroy his moral life. This is a fundamental moral principle.

But it doesn't mean all decisions of conscience are correct. Even with good will, one can be mistaken due to lack of knowledge or clarity or a wrong presentation of the problem. Other people, realizing our mistakes, must sometimes tell us where and how we went wrong. But they can't force us to see the situation that way, as if it were a mathematical problem.

Freedom of conscience must be defended—*the process by which each one comes to see what has to be done must be respected*—but it doesn't follow that all opinions are equally valuable or that everyone should be allowed to do whatever he wants. The interiority of conscience is inviolable, but external actions are not: intervention is allowable in regard to them. For instance, we can and must prevent a person from committing murder or suicide, even though he thinks it the right thing to do and doesn't understand why we object.

Conscience does not depend on likings but is meant to grasp reality. It is, then, subject to reason. Thus it is possible to explain abstractly what is right and what is wrong, which actions are according to order and which are disordered. This is something objective. It does not vary according to how each one sees it.

Not to respect our duties to God, neighbor, society, and nature is objectively bad. Loving our own goods without measure or in a disordered fashion is objectively bad. So is harming goods of our neighbor or preferring a personal good over a grave duty. All this we can know from reason.

And it is useful to know it because it helps form conscience. It is useful to know that murder, robbing, lying, lust, impure thoughts, fraud, envy, bribery, blasphemy, and insults are disorderly and bad actions. So it is useful to teach rationally about what is good and what is bad.

Even though actions can be judged in the abstract, however, it is difficult to judge them in concrete cases because they are often (though not always) very complex, with features difficult to evaluate from the outside. Thus we cannot and should not judge others by their actions since we cannot penetrate into their consciences. While sometimes it is good to judge actions by their objective aspects, from the outside (and certainly we must judge our own actions, because often we need to repent), in the end only God can judge accurately.

God judges from inside conscience. We can only judge from the outside. Morality or ethics supplies criteria for judging what we ought to be doing, not for judging others. Its main function is to direct our behavior.

Having a Right Conscience

The act of weighing what should be done, the judgment of conscience, depends on one's moral knowledge—goods and duties, the measure and order of different goods, the order of love.

We possess spontaneous knowledge of what is orderly and disordered, good or evil. Good actions appear beautiful, bad ones repugnant. Every normal person feels approval for someone who sacrifices himself to fulfill his duty and repugnance toward acts like murder, robbery, and lying. They may not be able to explain it, but people realize spontaneously that it's bad not to fulfill a promise (fail in a duty), to steal (harm the goods of one's neighbor), get drunk (lack measure in the desire of a good), or be selfish.

Approval and repugnance depend largely on intuitive recognition of the order or disorder of an action. That is to say, *they depend on the effect of evil seen as ugly and good as beautiful.* If the actions are disguised, the natural moral sense can go wrong.

Suppose you witness a murder. You're locked in a room and from the window can see a murderer stabbing a child. You see the blood, are aware of the child's suffering, hear his cries. You don't need convincing that what you've witnessed is very evil. You can see it is.

Now imagine you're in a Roman arena with a big crowd, shouting and enjoying the spectacle as a slave is released to a lion. When the lion attacks, the slave doesn't know what to do with the trident and tries to run away. Everybody laughs. And in those times we too would probably have laughed as the lion killed the slave. Lots of slaves died this way, and it didn't bother people. Slaves had no rights. They were punished severely for minor offenses. If one of them turned up in the arena, it meant he was dangerous or stole from his master or got drunk and beat other slaves.

Eventually someone who became accustomed to seeing slaves killed would probably have no longer had the sensitivity to perceive this as inhuman. But if someone recognized the slave as a friend or saw his child suffering, he would judge the situation differently, in a more humane way.

Acceptance of something so unnatural as abortion, the killing of a defenseless child, often derives from social pressure or from the mere fact that we haven't seen it happen—seen the torn bodies, screaming infants, chemical burns. Someone with minimal sensitivity needs to see an abortion only once to realize that it's an atrocity. The horror therefore is hidden in order to disguise the reality and numb the moral sense. "Interrupting pregnancy" and "killing an unborn baby" sound like different things!

Conscience can judge correctly only when the facts are clear and the order of goods and duties is recognized.

One's judgment is significantly influenced by society's valuing of things. Just as everyone living in the same time and place dresses, thinks, and behaves more or less like everyone else, so everyone tends to have similar opinion about values, with the same prejudices. The natural sense of good and evil can be modified in this way.

Normal people living in a civilized society who hear the screams of innocent victims realize that killing them is very bad. But people who live in a society accustomed to violence and have repeatedly been told why eliminating some individuals whom they neither see nor hear is advantageous, may not consider eliminating them so bad and may even believe it's something good.

The judgment of conscience depends on education and experience. To judge correctly, conscience needs principles and in-depth knowledge of the natural meaning of human actions—i.e., what goods and duties they involve.

The Ten Commandments

No one can attain moral knowledge fully by himself, since no one can have all the experience that would require. Thus an individual needs the moral experience of others to form his own conscience. In general, moral education comes from the culture we live in.

But this has problems. Human behavior involves frequent perplexities, imprecision, and error. As we have seen, there are disparities between the moral formulations of different cultures.

For this reason, there is also a *revealed morality*. Christians believe God has communicated the most important moral principles so that they will be accessible to everyone who wants to know them. This body of moral doctrine is presented in condensed form in the Decalogue, the Ten Commandments, which Moses received from God to be taught to the Jewish people.

People who consider morality something purely personal and private may regard this as unacceptable interference by God. But morality is not something private. It is based on the truth of things, and to be helped in the task of knowing the truth is not an insult.

The teaching of the moral law does not restrict conscience but illuminates it and allows it to judge securely and quickly. We must thank God for this guiding light. The creator of all things, who best knows the human heart, is the person best suited to teach what is fitting for man.

In these Ten Commandments we find a summary of the fundamental principles that rule human life. God wished to express them in a way suitable for the people he was dealing with, and so the formulation is very simple and easily understood. But, even so, they are an admirable compendium of life's wisdom.

The first three commandments concern our dealings with God.

I. "You shall worship the Lord your God, and him only shall you serve."

II. "You shall not take the name of the Lord your God in vain."

III. "Remember the Sabbath day, to keep it holy."*

The first and principal commandment is the axis of all morality. Other commandments, far from being a mere set of prohibitions, take their lead from the high and absolute moral ideal of loving God above all else.

The other seven commandments specify our duties to others.

IV. "Honor your father and your mother" (which in its widest sense points to the respect deserved by all authorities, as well as the veneration owed to parents).

V. "You shall not kill" (which prohibits harming the physical or moral person of our neighbors).

VI. "You shall not commit adultery" (which forbids the disorderly use of sexuality).

---

*Translator's note: in Spanish these commandments are expressed as follows:

I. "You shall love God above everything."

II. "You will not take the Name of God in vain."

III. "Sanctify the holy days."

VII. "You shall not steal" (which requires that we be just in our relations with others).

VIII. "You shall not bear false witness against your neighbor" (which insists that we live and always speak the truth).

IX. "You shall not covet your neighbor's wife" (which forbids evil desires and thoughts).

X. "You shall not covet your neighbor's possessions" (which rules out the desire to take the property of others or acquire it unfairly).

This is a simple code that people could learn by heart. It also is comprehensive—all morality is covered in these ten precepts. It can even be reduced to just two. In the Gospel of Matthew (22:37–39), Jesus says: "'You shall love the Lord your God with all your heart, and with all your soul, and with all your mind.' This is the great and first commandment. And a second is like it, 'You shall love your neighbor as yourself.'"

Some of the commandments are positive, saying what should be done; others are negative and state what must be avoided. But morality is not just about avoiding evil, which is the minimum. Morality consists above all in doing good. In a way, it's inexhaustible. The Ten Commandments teach us that human fulfillment is attained in coming to love God above all else and our neighbor as ourselves. This is the order of human loves.

4

Human Weakness

Weakness Experienced

"The moralities accepted among men may differ—though not so widely as is often claimed—but they all agree in prescribing a behavior which their adherents fail to practice. All men alike stand condemned, not by alien codes of ethics, but by their own, and all men therefore are conscious of guilt" (C.S. Lewis, *The Problem of Pain,* introduction). We are all sinners who violate our moral convictions, time and again failing to do the good we know we should do and doing the evil we should avoid.

So the mere fact of having a moral code or an ideal in life is not enough to live it. Everyone ends up violating his principles and ideals a little or a lot; nobody is entirely faithful.

The experience of freedom is universal: we think, decide, move, go wherever we want. Very often, though, someone who makes up his mind to do something slightly difficult doesn't do it. A man makes a firm decision to stop smoking, or go on a diet, or spend time jogging, or learn a new language—and he doesn't. It happens all the time. It's not that we've changed our minds or no longer want to do whatever it is. We just don't do it.

We haven't lost our freedom. But some sort of obscure not wanting arises—a free experience, so to speak, of failure of the will.

Someone who smokes after resolving to quit or who doesn't live up to his diet is aware of freely contradicting himself. Except for pathological cases of lack of will, the person could do what he proposed, but he just doesn't want to. He'd rather contradict himself freely. This is an experience of internal breakdown, of human weakness, of willing and not willing. It's as if something were broken inside.

Such human weakness doesn't take away our freedom but disrupts it. It is the weakness of a being who remains free. We're all weak, but some let themselves be carried further than others, some react immediately and others don't. The same person has times when he gives in easily and fails at everything, and times when he fights and triumphs, though never completely.

Weakness is bothersome, even humiliating. It has no cure except overcoming it each time it comes up.

Since every free action of a person leaves a trace, weakness increases whenever we yield and decreases whenever we conquer. A history of repeated failures can lead to the loss of liberty. In some areas this is quite clear: e.g., drug or alcohol addiction. In others, it's not as obvious but just as real: e.g., the slovenly lifestyle some people gradually adopt.

Boring from within like some sort of insect or worm, weakness undermines interior freedom. It takes away the strength to do as we ought. If we let it grow, it will destroy us in the end.

The Three Sources of Weakness

What makes us weak? What makes us do what we don't intend—or keeps us from doing what we meant to do? The causes are within us and, with slight variations, are the same in everyone.

We do what we didn't want to do when we let ourselves be carried away by goods to which we're attracted in a disorderly fashion—in the wrong way, at the wrong time, to the wrong extent. As for not doing what we should do, it has an even simpler interior explanation—we don't like effort, we're lazy.

Excessive love for goods and laziness are, then, interior causes of our weakness. But there is another, external cause: pressure from the culture. Such pressure affects our freedom, leading us to do what we did not desire, or not do what we wanted to do. Social pressure can have a beneficial educational effect, teaching us to behave like the rest and repressing eccentric, antisocial behavior; but in other cases it has a noxious influence, moving us to act contrary to what conscience tells us.

Let us look more clearly at these three sources of weakness: the disproportionate attraction of goods, laziness in regard to duties, and social pressure.

1) Attraction to goods is proper and desirable in that it helps us seek goods that improve us. But often goods attract us more than is proper, misleading us regarding what they offer, and giving rise to excessive expectations. We become fixed on them, even obsessive.

In some cases instincts impel us toward primary goods with disproportionate passion, moving us to desire them as or when they shouldn't be desired. Thus goods like food, drink, sex, comfort, and health can at times have an almost irresistible attraction.

In other cases, disorder lies in our liking for other goods, like work, money, social status, or sports. Having become very attractive, they take command of our feelings, so that we love them passionately and are unable to judge them objectively, while they distort conscience and cause us to be easily carried away.

Whenever we yield to disorder, our pre-existing weakness is reinforced. Love grows more disordered, we become more accustomed to yielding, our strength diminishes. Even as the desire for something (money, drugs, sex, food, comfort) increases, our satisfaction in having it decreases, while rash decisions become more likely.

All but the highest goods can be loved to excess, beyond reasonable measure. A disordered passion can develop for prestige, work, music, sports, collecting, or any other good. Some, such as gambling, alcohol, and drugs, are especially strong. To make correct decisions, we need to control the disproportionate attraction of goods and the accompanying disordered passions. That means strict observance of right order. Lacking that, someone who does not control his or her passions becomes, as it were, the puppet of his or her desires.

2) The other source of internal weakness is laziness. This is the reluctance to make the effort to comply with obligations. Here is the cause of so many excuses, delays, concessions, and work done poorly. And it's common, especially when fulfilling duty is difficult, involving few satisfactions and much monotony. Starting and finishing a job are moments of particular vulnerability.

Laziness has degrees. Some people are lazier than others. But achievement always is closely tied to a person's ability to overcome laziness. Nothing much will be accomplished otherwise.

Often this defect is not taken as seriously as it should be. It seems inoffensive. Surely not doing something good isn't as serious as doing something bad? But laziness is the cause of endless injustices. People in authority do not intervene to prevent evils or provide required services. Teachers do not teach what they should. Bureaucratic processes drag on forever, laws cease to operate, productivity declines.

Ambition and self-interest, though by no means necessarily admirable, do tend to militate against laziness. Laziness therefore is more likely to appear in regard to what should be disinterested activities: helping others, volunteer services, and the like. It is particularly strong in bureaucratic settings where people get paid whether they do their jobs or not. By contrast, those who have to please clients or customers have an incentive for working.

Classic economic liberalism holds that the promise of personal benefit is the only cure for this human tendency, and the evidence is that there's something to be said for this. A good salary, for instance, may be more of an incentive to give good service than a bad one. If used intelligently, the principle of self-interest can overcome laziness and lead to better services.

On the other hand, Christian morality holds that the true corrective of laziness—and the only truly noble one—is the spirit of service: commitment to direct one's personal activity to the service of others. Without denying the need to take self-interest into consideration, we must recognize that society should be governed by moral principles proper to human dignity. Exclusive reliance on self-interest would be appropriate to a colony of rats.

The inclination to seek the good for oneself is natural, but this tendency must be moderated through education to allow for the recognition of duty. We need to learn to do our duty, overcoming the resistance of laziness, and must teach young people to love that ideal of life as something good.

3) Besides these two interior sources of weakness, there is a third arising from *social pressure* or *peer pressure.* It is also called human respect and fear of ridicule. It makes us more timid, causes us to shape our behavior to suit the opinions of others for fear of drawing their disapproval.

While pressure from without is generally ill-defined and rather impersonal—not a purposeful coercion—people do respond to it. Unlike fear or respect for law and authority, this a response to unwritten laws and unrecognized authorities that often dominate us without our realizing it.

Everyone is affected this way. We think alike, dress alike, share the same idols and demons, believe that what everybody says is good is good, and what everybody says is bad is bad: *everybody does it, everybody thinks this way.*

This pressure can be seen at work in large numbers of people and small groups. Coercion from this source causes us to laugh at jokes that offend our beliefs and to be ashamed of our principles, our religion, our race, our origin, our profession, our family, or our friends. What's at work here is fear of not fitting in, being pointed at and singled out, becoming the butt of jokes or the object of contempt, being left alone and isolated.

Resisting this pressure means more than just sloughing off convention so as to draw attention to oneself. There may be good reasons why people all lean in the same direction, and a systematically contrarian response would be stupid. But sometimes there are no good reasons. Then we must stand up against uniformity and fads to defend our freedom.

The Effort to Overcome

Weakness in its three manifestations is an inseparable part of life. Overcoming it requires a *sporting approach*—a sustained effort to improve one's performance. And that involves conquering the false attractions that, entering the imagination, can take control of the mind.

Someone who wants to diet must avoid thinking about food all day, along with the occasions that give rise to such thoughts. (It would be stupid to keep an open box of chocolates constantly at hand.) This common-sense principle is called *fleeing the occasion.* And what is true of dieting is true in every field, from sobriety to fidelity in marriage. A passion not dominated can lead in time to great injustices, great misfortunes, and great remorse. Naïve romanticism may well end in tragedy.

When people are younger and more naïve, they tend to look askance at the idea of fleeing and avoiding the occasions. Isn't this cowardly? Wouldn't brave resistance be better? But those who think this way lack experience in the depth of human weakness. All the strength we can muster may not be enough to vanquish a temptation.

Disordered passion is bested by not allowing it to grow, not permitting it to seize control of the imagination, keeping it at bay, and repairing our defenses when they've been breached. It's often helpful training to deny ourselves what our feelings request, even though it be something good: not eating or drinking all we want, not satisfying curiosity, avoiding comfort, saying no to unnecessary expenditures, keeping to a schedule, doing the most important thing first even if we dislike doing it.

The point isn't to practice self-denial in everything always, but to do so in reasonable measure, and sometimes (when we've failed on another occasion) a little bit more. *The habit of limiting oneself, and tightening up to recover what has been lost, educates the feelings and protects freedom.*

Not only disorderly passions directed to various goods but other manifestations of weakness—laziness and human respect—require similar treatment. Although people who are naïve don't believe it, conquering the enemy requires clever use of our limited resources. It is very difficult to vanquish laziness and human respect if we entertain their arguments, let them fill our minds, permit them to weaken and reverse our decisions. Instead we must immediately do what we've seen needs doing, without excuses, second thoughts, and unplanned delays.

The fight against weakness can be summed up in this: *Be hard on yourself.* Not harsh, as a deranged person or masochist might be, but hard, with the studied and balanced hardness of a professional athlete bent on winning.

In this way we acquire habits for conquering ourselves by overcoming disordered passions, laziness, and social pressure. Such stable habits are *virtues*. They educate feelings, protect freedom, and help us do good, making life productive and beautiful.

Practices that moderate the excessive attraction of goods are expressions of *temperance*. To temper something is to regulate it, make it desirable, give it balance and serenity. This is just what happens in establishing order between feelings and duties. Under the general heading of temperance, sobriety limits food and drink, and chastity controls sexual desire.

Other things also must be ordered. We need to set limits to the desire to work, to prosper, to engage in hobbies and sports—everything that attracts us to excess. To be truly human, all must be governed by the measure of what is reasonable.

The virtue by which we vanquish interior difficulties (laziness) and exterior ones (social pressure) is called fortitude. *It is the capacity to force oneself to confront difficulties and overcome them.* In reference to laziness, we call it *strength of will*; in reference to external coercion or timidity, it is *courage, valor.* Fortitude comes into play not only in dramatic situations involving matters of great importance but also in regard to everyday things—punctuality, personal grooming, self-correction, working steadily. Courage is required to lead a good life and avoid what displeases God.

A life spent making demands on oneself may sound tedious, but this is an excellent and beautiful way to live. Life inevitably is filled with strife and effort, and without effort of the sort described here, there is no freedom in it. The struggle to repress evil is basic but more is required. The fundamental struggle of the moral life consists in discovering and loving higher goods, for herein lies the strength to draw upon the energies of freedom.

The Traces of Original Sin

Human weakness is not a superficial wound. It goes so deep that man can be called a deeply damaged being. A mysterious inconsistency deep within us prevents us from being what we should.

Superficial cures fall disastrously short of correcting the problem. Cravings for primary goods dominate us. Laziness persists. Disorder sprouts and grows.

People sometimes suppose that factual knowledge, clear thinking, and correct decisions will do the job. But the experience of individuals and nations all through history suggests otherwise. Modern science has not eliminated the absurdity of life, and our times have witnessed atrocities with no equal in prior history in magnitude, intensity, and number of peoples affected.

Obviously something is broken in the human person. But Christian teaching goes further and speaks of a mystery, *the mystery of original sin*, a congenital vice that damages the human condition. Our nature, our manner of being, is wounded from the beginning.

This sin of origin is a mystery, something hard to understand and accept. But without it there is no explaining what happens to man, while with it the mystery is illuminated and we see ways to deal with it. As Pascal says, "Man is more incomprehensible without this mystery, than the mystery itself is incomprehensible to man" (*Pensées*).

Original sin is not just a design fault like a physical deformity. It is a moral wound that affects our relationship with what is true and good. It is a strange and persistent inclination toward not doing what we should, and doing what we should not: absurd, illogical, unreasonable—but real and persistent.

Christian tradition, describing the permanent effects of original sin, points to four ruptures: with God, within ourselves, with other people, and with nature.

1) *The rupture with God* can be seen in the difficulty of entering into contact with him. What we are able to know of God is diminished, and we have a strange tendency to flee from him. T.S. Eliot remarked that human beings cannot tolerate "too much reality." We are fearful of God and seek to hide from him. The account of original sin in Genesis says that after sinning, Adam and Eve were ashamed and hid from God. But this conflicts with our natural tendency toward happiness that can be satisfied only in God.
2) *The internal rupture of the human person* shows itself in various ways: the ease with which we deceive ourselves about what we need to do, the lack of coherence between spirit and feelings, the readiness of the latter to override the will and darken conscience, the impotence of will when it comes to imposing and executing its decisions. All these problems come together in conscience.
3) Original sin is manifested also in *divisions among men.* Misunderstandings seem to proliferate the closer people are to one another. Relationships among relatives and neighbors are easily poisoned. People take perverse pleasure in making life difficult for others. Forgiving is difficult, grudges accumulate, we seek revenge. These tendencies are acted out on a vast scale all through history. Scripture's iconic representation of this tendency is the tower of Babel, where language itself became an instrument for separating peoples.
4) Finally, there is *a rupture between man and the whole of nature.* Nature can at times appear inhospitable and threatening. Sickness, pain, and death are universal realities of human existence.

These four ruptures are not mere shortcomings. They have a malignant dimension, an element of perversity—a profound distortion of reality, an inversion of truth, goodness, and beauty. History records recurring episodes of systemic irrationality, hatred and persecution of good people, a cult of the perverse expressed in violence, sadism, and ruthlessness. Beauty is held in contempt, what is degraded and disgusting is esteemed, the divine is driven out and its symbols shattered. At such moments it is hard not to see strange, unnatural forces at work.

The world, it appears, is alarmingly open to these manifestations of perversion. Scripture calls the Devil both Lord of the World and Father of Lies, and his influence cannot be excluded as the explanation of some historical events and deeds. Human weakness is not the only destructive force at work shaping history.

Christian doctrine teaches that these four ruptures render us incapable of doing all the good we should do by our own power.

Without special help from God, we cannot be faithful to conscience, cannot heal the deep wounds of sin. This help has a name, grace, meaning "a free gift of God." *Grace is the strength of God acting inside us*, helping us introduce the order of intelligence into our feelings and behavior, and moving us to be faithful to God's will. It is a mysterious reality with power to transform human life. The Church has a rich experience of such transformations.

Our minds need this external aid—this grace—to heal the original wound. Grace corrects disorder and sows love of higher and more beautiful goods, with a preference for what is great. We shall return to this later.

Moral wisdom is acquired only with the help of grace. Only with God's assistance can we acquire sound moral knowledge, right desires that reject selfishness and move us to love God and neighbor, and power to overcome our weakness.

Perfection is beyond our reach in this life, but Christians believe it will be attained in the end, when all things are incorporated into Christ. Meanwhile we must strive as athletes do, seek God's grace, and look for it where he has placed it—in those mysterious channels of grace called the sacraments, where the Church recapitulates the mysteries of Christ's life and death.

5

The Horizon of Freedom

Living in the Truth

Human beings have a visible freedom and invisible one. A person is visibly free who does as he or she wants, without being compelled or impeded. Free persons can come and go, live wherever they choose, have their own opinions, travel, meet people, live as they prefer. The more important part of freedom is, however, the part we don't see. This *interior freedom* is the freedom of conscience. Those who are internally free can direct themselves by the light of conscience, unimpeded by interior obstacles.

Yet conscience does have obstacles: ignorance and weakness. Someone who does not know what ought to be done is free to make mistakes but lacks the freedom to be right; while the freedom of a weak man or woman is taken from him or her by disordered feelings or the pressure of other people's opinions.

Ignorance silences the voice of conscience. A conscience that is malformed or has limited moral formation is consistently off-target. People in this state aren't really exhibiting freedom of conscience in the way they behave. Not having been taught to appreciate goods like beauty, friendship, and culture, they are, practically speaking, unaware of the goods' existence and without the freedom to reach them.

Weakness darkens conscience. A gambling addict will make poor decisions about the use of time because passion gets the better of him. A lazy man ignores his duties, puts off doing them, deceives himself, and forgets them in the end. A woman dominated by peer pressure is unable to do things others may criticize. People like these are free only to do what is wrong.

To be internally free, one must overcome ignorance and the various expressions of weakness. A well-functioning conscience is required in order to discover the truth and establish proper order between goods and duties.

To form conscience, one must try to know moral principles, seek advice from upright, experienced persons, and humbly accept correction. One must also know how to learn from what one does, examining one's behavior often, even daily, evaluating it, and correcting errors, both practical and theoretical. This is the way to wisdom that in time makes us able to help others.

Conscience is in play in every decision we make. Either we act by its truth or we shunt it aside and silence it. In the first case, we are the ones who act, with a nucleus of freedom directing our conduct. In the second, some part of us—likings, laziness, fear of what others will say—makes us hardly more than a bundle of tendencies competing to dominate us.

If we are faithful to what conscience sees, virtues grow. As they do, the reach of conscience expands and our interior freedom grows. This is the virtuous circle of our perfection.

But the opposite also can happen. When we act against conscience, weakness increases and freedom is lost. This is the vicious circle of increasing interior disintegration. It is imperative to halt the process, repent, and start over again as often as necessary.

The loss of the light of conscience is the gravest of diseases. While not a physical illness, it is a real disease that destroys the inner nucleus of the personality, suppressing interior freedom and causing one to live in a state of falsehood. Avoiding it requires rectifying our behavior whenever necessary.

But because it's humiliating to admit we've gone wrong, we tend to justify our wrong actions, even in theory. As Cicero said, "In a heart rotten by passions we always find hidden reasons to consider false what is true. . . . We convince ourselves easily of what we want, and when the heart subjects itself to the seduction of pleasure, the mind rests in the arms of the lies that justify it" (*De Natura Deorum*, I, 54).

The deception can reach pathological levels when weakness is associated with pride. Truth annoys the proud man, and he is even annoyed by those who live according to truth. St. Augustine says: "When one loves something which is not the truth, he pretends to himself that what he loves is the truth, and because he hates to be proved wrong, he will not allow himself to be convinced that he is deceiving himself. So he hates the real truth for the sake of what he takes to his heart in its place." (*Confessions*, X, 23). Twisted people reach the point of persecuting the good with irrational violence. This is the source of much of the intolerance and injury inflicted on good people.

A person who always follows his or her conscience is said to be *upright.* This quality gives life extraordinary beauty and makes one who possesses it master of his actions.

To live in agreement with conscience is to live in truth. Thus a great love of truth is a sign of uprightness. Upright people have a profound aversion to lies. To lie out of fear of truth's consequences is like being without a conscience.

The Place of Freedom

Moral doctrine involves both negative precepts ("thou shall not . . .") marking the minimal threshold of morality, and also positive ones, like the commandment to love God above all things and one's neighbor as oneself. These positive commandments mark out permanent goals for the whole of life.

Morality is not a legal code, a list of what's good and bad. That is the role of conscience. Morality points out a framework, within which there is ample room for creativity. But even so, freedom is not absolute. Rather, it is strongly conditioned by all that precedes it: the laws of nature, the things and persons around us. It is *freedom in a place.*

Freedom in a Place

First of all, *we are limited by our own nature.* This elementary fact is very important in considering what to do with freedom. Moreover, we need to consider our individual circumstances—talents, intelligence, inclinations, capabilities, health, weaknesses, physical defects.

Many other things also condition us and situate us in the world: where we live and work, and especially the people around us—parents, siblings, children, kin, friends, co-workers, neighbors, and many others. It would be stupid to reject these persons and things and circumstances or feel ashamed of them. They define us in many ways. Someone with a sick parent can't ignore the fact. Someone responsible for caring for a family can't make important decisions as if the family didn't exist. Daydreaming about what one would do in different circumstances is a waste of time, a flight into a fantasy world.

Freedom without limits is likewise a fantasy. Limitations are, to some extent, the starting point of the game that makes it so exciting. In fact, there would be no game without them. Each one must play the game within his own particular framework—with the cards he's been dealt.

The things around us impose duties, usually pleasant ones and easy to live with. Only people who think freedom means not having anything to do that must be done will find this a drag. In reality, it's rewarding to have a country, a city, parents, siblings, friends, neighbors.

Soon of course, one confronts a recurring question: *How shall I respond to the voices of my duties?* From the time a child starts to recognize duties, he or she must make continuous choices. Keep watching the movie or do the chore mother has asked me to do? The interplay of goods and duties has begun.

At first, only goods are considered, but then conscience appears and declares that duty takes precedence—the chore must be done. This situation recurs over and over, in different ways. Conscience must decide which good or duty should be preferred. At the end of the game, someone who heeds conscience most of the time is a real man; someone who usually disobeys finishes as a wretch.

Getting up when you'd prefer to stay in bed, helping your mother in the kitchen when you'd rather watch TV, listening to what your spouse wants to tell you instead of reading a magazine—these and countless other everyday situations represent the priority of duty over personal preference. *Deciding rightly is the only therapy for selfishness.* Selfishness diminishes only when we listen to the voice of duty, summoning us out of ourselves and leading us to care for others.

Usually it is easy to see who is selfish and who is noble. A selfish person is mainly concerned with his or her goods. An upright person sacrifices goods (comfort, time, energy, money, and so on) to fulfill a duty—often a duty to another person or persons.

There are different ways of fulfilling duty. One can have a passionate, generous love for duty, or one can approach it in a stoic (or Kantian) mode (I do this because I should). A man can take his wife for a walk with the enthusiasm of a criminal on death row or the enthusiasm of a loving husband. The wife can listen to her husband talking football with stoic impassiveness or with affection. Precisely because we are free, we can surpass ourselves and do more than the minimum. Everyone has his or her own style of fulfilling duties.

Other elements of personal style are visible in the selection of goods that interest us. One can seek a few earthly goods or aim at the highest goods, choose among aesthetic, religious, and cultural goods, personal relationships, and so on. To a great extent, freedom is at work in these choices.

The choices of style are a great field for exercising freedom and developing habits that will endow one's conduct with beauty and nobility.

The Great Choices

Everyone is different, with different limitations, different degrees of freedom, and different life situations. The idea is expressed in the parable of the talents in chapter 25 of the Gospel of Matthew. "Talent" now refers to a natural gift or skill, but originally it was a weight, a measure, of money—gold or silver talents. The parable in Matthew tells of a rich man who, before leaving on a trip, distributed talents to his employees to be administered: five to one of them, two to another, only one to the third— "to each according to his ability."

"He who had received the five talents went at once and started trading with them; and he made five talents more. Similarly, he who got the two talents made two more. But he who had received the one talent went and dug a hole in the ground and hid his master's money." When the master returned, he demanded an accounting. The one who had earned five talents was congratulated. So was the one who earned two. But the one with only one talent to show was sharply rebuked: "You wicked and slothful servant! . . . You ought at least to have invested my money with the bankers, and at my coming I should have received what was my own with interest." The master expelled him from his presence.

The parable has an obvious meaning. Each of us receives certain possibilities and capacities with which to "trade." Some spend their lives daydreaming about what they will do—someday. Some grow vain because they are intelligent, or because of their family's power or wealth, or because of their ability in sports, music, or business, or because they are considered good looking. They spend their time showing off, without considering that their talents were given them to bear fruit.

Talents increase the ability to do what we want, and that is an advantage, but it also carries with it a *responsibility.* We shall have to give an accounting for what we did with what we received.

In earlier times, most people had a limited area for the exercise of freedom. They were largely determined by the circumstances of their birth and culture. A serf's life, for instance, was to a considerable extent a given. Today, at least in developed countries, most young people can decide how they will use their time and energies. To hold so much of the direction of one's life in one's hands is obviously a talent. Never before have so many been able to decide so freely about themselves.

Of course the choices must be made in a timely fashion. One shouldn't fear to commit oneself, and delaying may mean a wasted life, the life of a perpetual adolescent. Mature people devote their lives to something worthwhile.

So we must choose. It may be painful to abandon other possibilities, but choice is the only path to accomplishment. In choosing, it is necessary to consider things realistically, without looking for ideal conditions that don't exist. One must become informed and choose among real possibilities, according to one's knowledge, inclinations, tastes, and ability, which also are talents. Since there's usually more than one possibility, it's necessary to proceed in stages—education or training first, then the actual work.

But avoid the kind of self-fulfillment literature that speaks as if happiness could only be found in realizing some marvelous destiny. Naïve and sentimental thinking like that leads to perpetual dissatisfaction. People who expect some day to be recognized as geniuses are dreaming. There is a limited demand for geniuses, and much competition. One's desires should be focused on service to others, love in the family, love for one's work, and love of God, not on naïve, selfish imaginings. This doesn't mean ignoring likings and inclinations. It means serving God and others with our inclinations and likings, work, and use of free time, as well as all our other talents: position, prestige, money, influence.

Successive commitments modify the framework of our freedom and give rise to new obligations. This is not to be feared. Commitments made with love will make us happy. This is how people usually find fulfillment.

Other choices, ours and others', also modify our freedom. Gabriel Marcel speaks of *encounters*: those moments when we meet someone who will become part of our life, moments when friendship or love is born.

Each encounter is a grace, a gift, something unexpected, one senses that it has been prepared from the beginning. It may be with our future spouse, with a friend, or with God. God, too, comes into many people's lives as an encounter, something prepared long ago and pointing to eternity.

These joyful encounters light up life and lead to huge changes, creating strong bonds and modifying the framework of our lives. We should not be afraid of those commitments, since it is by these commitments of love, these acts of self-giving, that one fulfills oneself and achieves happiness. *Without love—without encounter—there can be no happiness.*

Heroism and Beauty

Imagine you live in a country with an oppressive and tyrannical government, where civil rights are ignored and terror reigns. One day you meet an old friend whom you haven't heard from in a long time. He tells you he was sent to jail and kept in dehumanizing conditions. He escaped that hell only by cooperating, and giving information about several companions.

You have followed his story with sympathy, but at this point your feelings freeze. You can't be certain you would have acted differently—but how painful to hear that someone you love has informed on his friends. If only he'd resisted! Then you would love him much more, seeing him as a hero, a model, an example to imitate. But an informer? You may still feel a certain friendship for him, even love, but that weakness of his is a failing you must struggle to forgive.

Sometimes human dignity calls on people to make great sacrifices, in other words, to practice *heroism.* Duty may call on us to face pain and death rather than yield to something beneath a human being. Primary goods, like life itself, clearly are not the most important ones.

In view of our own weakness, none of us is in a position to reproach others for failing to respond heroically to various circumstances. Yet human dignity demands that we not yield in those situations. And we have a duty to remind others of that. Our common humanity would be disgraced if no one were capable of living and dying with dignity.

But can we ask a soldier to defend a strategic position with his life? A fireman to risk his life to save a child? A captain to be last to abandon a sinking ship? A doctor to treat a patient with an infectious disease? A policeman to risk his life to free a hostage?

In all these examples, there is some duty, either freely assumed or natural, that in particular circumstances can call for the supreme sacrifice. No individual can demand it, but human dignity can. We can understand and excuse the cowardice of those who can't measure up, but measuring up would be better, and we must aspire to that if we find ourselves in the same situation.

History is filled with the exemplary deeds of people who sacrificed themselves in light of higher duties—the good of the homeland, the love of parents, wife, children, friends. Where most people would have thrown in the towel, they didn't and we admire them for it.

There is beauty in such gestures. A Jewish woman had the opportunity to avoid being seized and taken to Auschwitz, but she refused. Instead, she chose to accompany her father there because he was deaf and she feared that, not hearing the guard's commands, he would be beaten. It was at Auschwitz, too, that Father Maximilian Kolbe gave up his life in place of another prisoner with children. "Those of us who were in concentration camps," recalls Viktor Frankl, "remember those men who went from barrack to barrack, consoling the others and giving their last crust of bread. They may have been few in number, but they were sufficient proof that everything can be taken away except one thing, the last human freedom" (*Man's Search for Meaning*).

In a consumer society such behavior may seem naïve since it involves sacrificing immediate goods. But consider: Should we teach the young that everyone should keep his eye only on what benefits him—with "benefit" understood basely? In fact, there is no greater benefit for a person than being allowed to sacrifice himself or herself for an ideal. But morality that attaches more value to private benefit than to the common good is a morality of contempt for humanity.

Only a human being can prefer duty to what instincts dictate. Other creatures simply act for the sake of their own immediate goods, but humans are capable of sacrificing themselves for goods more valuable than life.

Such choices do not occur only in extraordinary circumstances. We are constantly being faced with choices between desires—inclinations, laziness—and duty. The mature individual postpones the satisfaction of desire and does his or her duty.

Love is the natural school of this heroic behavior. Countless men and women who never theorize about love nevertheless live heroically each day by selflessly satisfying the demands of their love for parents, children, husband or wife, friends, or native land. Love moves us to love our duty as our good. Where morality is perfect, goods and duties are one.

PART II

RESPECT

The five chapters that follow deal separately with relationships: with nature and material goods (6), other people (7), sexual morality (8), society (9), and God (10).

The heading "respect" recalls Dietrich von Hildebrand's observation that the fundamental attitude of morality is respect for the realities around us. Living with the dignity proper to a human being requires that we know the truth about our surroundings (part I of this book) and live according to it (part II).

6

Administrator but Not Owner

Consumption, or Respect for Nature

It is part of Christian doctrine that God has placed man in charge of creation to care for it and use it for his needs. This is clear from the book of Genesis and its symbol-filled account of the creation of the world and humankind. Here is the basis for the relationship of man and things. Humans are not only to use things but also care for them. Things belong to God. Man is only an administrator and will have to give an accounting of what has been entrusted to him.

At times in the past, and especially during the Industrial Revolution, it was common to treat nature as if it were inexhaustible and could be exploited indefinitely. This mentality, which still exists (though perhaps without being as visible as it once was), tends to consider nature as *res nullius*, "nobody's property." Typically, it leads to gorging on things, like a child trying to stuff himself on a whole chocolate cake, oblivious to the bad results that may have.

This way of thinking is especially immoral in our times for two reasons. First, the means of exploiting and transforming nature are more powerful than ever before, and the harm done is correspondingly greater. Second, our understanding of the world is clearer. For example, we know that natural resources are limited, and while some can be regenerated, some cannot. The harm done in exhausting the latter is thus irreparable.

Man has greater dignity than the rest of material creation, but things also have dignity that we must respect. We can, and should, use nature to satisfy our needs, but we must treat it well, much as we care for our own homes.

What does it mean to care for nature? Many things. First, by not destroying it. It is immoral to use nonregenerating natural resources to the point of exhausting them (e.g., fossil fuels and the ecosystem indispensable to the survival of particular species of animals and plants). It is immoral to squander resources when we could do with less. It is immoral to destroy anything in nature just for the pleasure of destroying it.

On the other hand, as those entrusted with caring for the earth, we must seek to mitigate the self-destructive elements present in nature: earthquakes, forest fires, volcanic eruptions, and so forth.

Beyond all utilitarian considerations, however, nature has the peculiar dignity of being a reflection of God, a reflection of divine goodness. This is something we should respect, protect, and maintain.

Consider garbage. Human activity unavoidably produces garbage. But when human beings act carelessly and disrespectfully, they produce it in a disproportionate and destructive measure.

Garbage is more than something hauled away by sanitation workers. It is also an abandoned quarry, an excavation that goes unfinished, debris thrown by the side of a road. Every trace of human carelessness in nature is garbage—an insult to creation.

We are called to add beauty to creation, not remove it. This beauty, the fruit of human intelligence, is of many kinds: great art and great technical prowess, good urban architecture, productive farming and mining, quarries and highways. All reflect intelligent order.

But order is generated only through disorder. Building a car, for instance, requires tons of raw materials. Each step in the process generates a certain amount of industrial debris, and each automobile represents significant manipulation of nature. The same is true of everything we use (buildings, highways, and all the rest).

Today the consumerism found in developed countries poses an unprecedented threat to nature. Never before have so many goods been produced and so many things sold. And never before has surplus been such a problem. Even worse is the manner in which things are consumed, with new things produced to take the place of older ones for no good reason but with further manipulation of nature.

As individuals, our response should be to prefer a sober style of life. Don't have superfluous or unnecessary things, try to make things last, repair old things instead of discarding them—and in these ways make a small dent in the production of garbage.

In our culture of abundance, the proliferation of garbage points to a simple truth: the consumption of nature is excessive. Morality requires that we flee consumerism and adopt a more sober lifestyle for nature's sake. People in earlier times didn't know this. We have no excuse for not knowing it.

Our Relationship with Things

One false way of relating to things might be called human voraciousness. At the heart of it is an irrational desire to possess—irrational because it lacks measure.

Voraciousness ignores the nature of things. It is the opposite of the *contemplative spirit,* which looks at things, not wanting to possess them, in order to enjoy their beauty while keeping a certain distance. Some people enjoy a tree, a house, objects of all sorts, only when and insofar as they are theirs. Others enjoy trees, houses, and other things because they appreciate their beauty and grace. In the first instance, what matters is owning things; in the second their own dignity is valued.

Ownership is a necessary part of life, but there are diverse relationships with things owned. One style of ownership manifests contempt for things, another appreciates them, and a third involves being owned by things.

1) Start with ownership that does not respect the dignity of things. It fails to distinguish the individuality of things. One car is the same as another—and so too with everything else, houses, trees, whatever it might be. A man like this doesn't care if things break down, since they can always be replaced. This mentality leads to carelessness and squandering. Things are mistreated, lose their dignity and usefulness, become garbage. The external surroundings in which some people live reflect this attitude toward things.

It can happen to rich people as well as to the poor. But, regardless of income, order and cleanliness and even good taste are, genuine indigence aside, possible with a little more effort, inasmuch as human persons are intelligent beings.

At a certain level of affluence, however, negligence can be concealed by spending. At this level, too, it is common for owners to replace old things with new ones merely for the sake of having what's new.

This is a frivolous and even immoral mentality. It gives rise to much more consumption than necessary, irrational exploitation of natural resources, and the proliferation of garbage. It also expresses a lack of human solidarity, visible in the gross contrast between unleashed consumerism and the extreme poverty present in other societies.

2) What does respect for things really mean? First of all, recognizing their dignity, the fact that they are not merely instruments. Here is an entire philosophy, the very antithesis of the dehumanization present in mass-produced things.

To respect things means using them according to what they are—respecting their way of being and, in the case of man-made instruments, using them as intended. Respecting things also requires taking good care of them, keeping them in good repair and presentable in appearance, repairing them promptly when repairs are needed.

There's an old saying that throwing out bread is a sin. That may be a stretch, but throwing bread away is certainly insensitive at a time when so many people die of hunger.

3) Finally, there is the way of owning that is more like being owned. Its name is avarice or greed. This is the attitude of one who cannot contemplate things, but is overcome by the desire to have them and pursues them compulsively.

Of course, there is an orderly desire for goods. We need food, housing, and many other useful things that make life pleasant. But there is also a disordered desire: one desires things that will not be used or enjoyed. Then the desire to possess occupies so much of a person's time that there is no time left for higher goods.

Love of Money

A disordered tendency to own is usually expressed in the love of money. Money is not properly a good, but a conventional means of exchange that enables us to acquire real goods. Thus it gives rise to a peculiar kind of avarice not centered on goods but on the means of getting them. The love of money is the most pure form of avarice: desire to own without real content, without concrete goods. It is like loving ownership itself.

Plainly one cannot live in a developed society without money. But we need to ask ourselves how much money we really need and what else besides money is important.

Money is not the most important thing. It is *an instrument.* We need to know why we want it, how much it cost us to get it, how much we need. Then we can leave time and energy free for pursuing important goods like culture, religion, and human relationships.

In some cases, however, as people age they come to believe that making money is the only important thing in life. It's as if other things from which they once expected much (love, travel, culture, and so on) had faded and only money kept its value. Such people often regard any other view of life as foolish or eccentric. But this is nonsense that ignores a fundamental fact: everyone dies, and no one gets to take his money with him—and it would be useless to him if he did. St. Augustine says: "Neither we, nor our children get to be happy through earthly riches. . . . Only God makes us happy, because He is the true riches of the soul" (*City of God,* V, 18, 1).

Money provides only things and services that can be bought. It does not provide peace of soul or teach us to enjoy beauty or friendship or the warmth of love or the small delights of family life or give us the ability to savor small everyday events or an encounter with God. It does not provide intelligence or knowledge. It does not supply virtue or make people good mothers and fathers, good public officials, good Christians.

Money and the important goods are not necessarily opposed, they are simply different things. Except in extreme cases of great poverty or great wealth, having or not having money is irrelevant to love, friendship, honesty, and any other good.

At the same time, a minimum of material goods is usually necessary to attain spiritual goods. It is difficult to think of other goods when one lives in misery and dirt, when the necessities of survival are not guaranteed. Furthermore, material misery often brings with it other human problems including social exclusion, irresponsibility, the deterioration of personal, familial, and societal structures, and corruption.

On the other hand, excess also has problems. When the love of money replaces the love one should have for God and neighbor, the problem at its roots is not money but the disorder of one's love.

We need to give love of money its proper place in the scale of things we love, and since it's not the most important thing, that place can't be the first. It is a disorder to devote so much time to making money that there's no time for other goods—friendship, family, rest, our relationship with God, culture.

But money can be placed before higher goods almost without one's noticing: for example, by spending too much time working to provide for one's children when what they need most is their parent's companionship. The breakup of families in inheritance disputes is another sad instance. Brothers and sisters come to hate one another for a few shares of stock, a bit of land, houses, furniture.

Having a lot of money is neither morally good nor bad. It has advantages and disadvantages. Among the latter is a tendency to corrupt. People who love money too much are often easily bought for the sake of luxuries they don't need.

It isn't easy to be rich and honest. Christ said it is harder for a rich man to get to heaven than for a camel to pass through the eye of a needle. The Lord then adds: "For men it is impossible, but not for God, because all things are possible with God." To be rich *and* a good Christian requires a great deal of help from God.

The disadvantages of riches are now widespread in wealthy countries. Vanity, whim, luxury, frivolity, and corruption once accessible to only a few are now within the reach of the masses.

But being rich also has advantages. The least important is that basic needs are easily satisfied. The advantages most important from a moral perspective expand the possibilities for the use of freedom. To be rich brings with it great freedom to do good. It is a "talent," a responsibility. The key issue is the service that wealth enables a person to provide. And that calls for an appropriate lifestyle.

The Economist Mentality

The moral criteria that apply to individuals in their use of money also apply to society. Social life is more than economic life, even though many people imagine otherwise and suppose government's main function is to provide for the material welfare of its citizens.

Economics is the science of using resources and material goods properly. Even within the economic sphere, we cannot operate as if money were the primary good. Economic life is lived by people who need other goods besides merely economic ones.

At times it is difficult to keep this in mind. Modern economics has become a highly abstract discipline, with a strong mathematical underpinning. Mathematics by nature tends to disguise reality, since it can consider only things that can be measured. But behind the numbers are persons, human relationships, cultural, religious, and artistic needs that cannot be expressed in numbers and so may be overlooked even as the mathematical models lead us to forget the moral decisions underlying economic trends.

As Pope John Paul II repeatedly pointed out, however, persons are always more important than things. It is a disorder, an immorality, to make economic decisions without considering how they will affect the persons involved. Businesses are businesses, and persons are persons.

Classical liberal economic thinking places great emphasis on the law of supply and demand as a fundamental principle of a free market. Everything revolves around it: raw materials, machinery, manufactured goods, transport, services, and manpower, the human factor. Even though manpower is not merchandise, the economic system treats it as if it were—merchandise offered and paid for in the market as a cost of production.

7

Your Neighbor as Yourself

Among Equals

People are fundamentally equal. Not equal in looks, clothing, sense of humor, way of thinking, history, or aspirations. But equal in being people like oneself.

Here is the basis for the second part of the Decalogue, summed up as "Love your neighbor as yourself." If people are our equals, it only makes sense to love them as we love ourselves. This is the foundation of justice: we are equally people; we all have the same rights as persons; we should all treat one another as equals.

But besides pointing out that we are equal, the commandment says we must love one another. Of course that is not the only possibility: From a naturalistic point of view, equality might be the starting point for competition, life according to the law of the jungle.

Lest this happens, laws are adopted guaranteeing everyone at least the minimum needed to survive. Making the laws work and correcting abuses is the government's job. Yet even in developed societies, the law of the jungle may be in operation outside the reach of the law.

And in the end of course it is impossible to make people love their neighbor as a matter of law. Charity cannot be imposed from outside. It is a matter of morality, which requires the personal exercise of freedom.

Thus the moral precept "you shall love your neighbor as yourself" goes far beyond respecting the law and the fundamental rights of others, although these things are part of it. To love means to desire the good of one's neighbor, not just to avoid harming or inconveniencing him or her. True solidarity is required. To love always means giving, or at least the disposition to give: in a way, to give oneself. Things do not deserve our love, but people do. We have to love our brothers and sisters.

And we must do that for the fundamental reason that they are people. Not because they are tall or short, black or white, poor or rich, or because we like something they have. We must love them for what they are: human beings. That includes those we find not so easy to love—the weak, the sick, the needy, those who are unpleasant, unfair, wrong-doers. We don't love the evil they do, but their human condition. As for the evil, we must hate it and would gladly have it eliminated—because we love those who do it.

Goods and Evils of Our Neighbor

What goods are we supposed to desire for our neighbors and what evils should we help them avoid?

The Christian principle tells us to wish for our neighbor what we wish for ourselves and not wish for them what we don't care to have. Instinctively, we are quick to recognize what goods help us and what evils harm us, and that should teach us how to treat others.

The first good we desire is *life and physical integrity.* We have to wish this for everybody and avoid what may harm them. Any attempt against another person's life is gravely immoral, as is any aggression that can harm his health: blows, abuse, mutilations.

Only in self-defense may we harm another person—not to injure him, but because of our right to preserve our life and integrity. The response must be proportionate to the threat: we cannot strike the first blow or respond by doing more injury needed to repel the attack. If someone slaps you, you can't shoot him. Nor is it allowed to seek revenge. One may have a right to reparation, but not by inflicting a similar damage. Punishment may be licit, even necessary, since it may have educational value, but never vengeance. The duty to impose licit punishment resides with those who have authority to punish.

We all desire to keep our health and enjoy the minimal goods necessary for survival. Thus we cannot be indifferent while so many people live below minimal levels. Distant people are our neighbors. And although it may be difficult to do much, one must do what one can—supporting organizations for relief and development, encouraging solidarity among nations and persons, perhaps volunteering one's services, avoiding a wasteful lifestyle.

Pockets of poverty exist even in developed societies, and the problems of the very poor often are extremely difficult to solve inasmuch as they lack the necessary work attitudes and knowledge. As a rule, caring for these cases is a job for specialized organizations; government may operate with more or less success. But even though we cannot do very much, we cannot be indifferent. To the extent possible, we should try to see that everyone (beginning with those who depend on us) has what is required for minimum material welfare: food, clothing, and housing.

Private property is a desirable good. Ownership increases the sense of responsibility, reinforces personality, and multiplies a person's options.

But property rights are not absolute. Although they are principles of order, they carry less weight than what is called "the universal destination of goods" (to which at times they must yield). We should do whatever we can to ensure the equitable distribution of material and spiritual goods.

Society benefits when there are many owners. Concentration of ownership abets abuse and the misuse of goods, whereas things are better cared for and productivity is enhanced where ownership is widespread. Government and the private sector should both foster ownership.

Stealing is an assault against human dignity and demands restitution. One who has stolen something should return it or its equivalent to the owner. Note that there are many ways of stealing besides breaking into a safe. Deceiving a customer to get his business, violating a patent, obtaining a contract by bribery, underselling smaller competitors to put them out of business, failing to provide a contracted service, delivering less of something or of lower quality than promised—these are all forms of stealing.

Material things are not the only kind of goods. Everyone enjoys a patrimony of immaterial goods that can be damaged.

Honor is one. It directly affects people's dignity. Even when they don't seem to deserve it, everybody has the right to be treated as a person—not shouted at, not shamed, not insulted, humiliated or abused, but treated with consideration and kindness.

Courtesy expresses the respect people deserve. It consists of practices like saying please and thank you, addressing others in a pleasant tone, paying attention to what they say. No one should be made to feel assaulted, disgraced, or out of place.

This is particularly important when dealing with subordinates. We should treat them as we would like to be treated. It is a good practice to imagine ourselves in their place.

Another important immaterial good is the good opinion of others—that is, one's good name. It is immoral to criticize somebody out of spite or simply out of frivolity or a desire to gossip. Even when gossip is true, it is still immoral. A neighbor's defect should not be revealed without a substantial reason. To do so is defamation—or, if not true, calumny, which is more serious than stealing, since reputation is worth more than money.

At times, it may be necessary to tell something to a person's discredit, as, for example, when reporting his misconduct to someone who can correct it or saying whether a person is qualified for a job. Then we must tell the truth. But we still must treat others as we would like to be treated, preferring an explanation that stresses good intentions and shows understanding for weaknesses.

Always of course we should wish for our neighbors the greater goods—human formation, culture, a job, knowledge of the truth, human relationships like friendship and love. And we must desire that they encounter God, which is the greatest good.

One finds a classic summary of good deeds that should be done for neighbors in the works of mercy. The list is divided into two segments of seven each. Some may seem out of date today, but all are worth pondering.

The first seven works of mercy are called *corporal*:

Visiting and caring for the sick.

Feeding the hungry.

Giving drink to the thirsty.

Sheltering the homeless.

Clothing the naked.

Redeeming captives.

Burying the dead.

The *spiritual* works of mercy are:

Teaching the ignorant.

Giving good advice to whoever needs it.

Correcting those in error.

Forgiving injuries.

Consoling the sad.

Suffering with patience the defects of our neighbors.

Praying to God for the living and the dead.

Our Closest Neighbors

Keeping one's word is *fidelity.* A faithful man is a man of his word.

There are many kinds of pacts in life—commercial, political, and so on. In some, like friendship and marriage, what people commit are themselves.

In principle, pacts should be equitable, with a certain correspondence between what is given and received. It is wrong to exploit a neighbor's problems to impose an undesirable deal—buying a house for less than it's worth because the owner urgently needs the money, hiring someone for less than what is just because he or she desperately needs a job. Even if the other party agrees, it is wrong to violate his or her dignity. (On the other hand, organized workers may not demand that their employers operate at a loss, since that would not be equitable, either.)

Friendship and matrimony are special commitments between persons giving rise to duties of fidelity. The duties are especially serious in the case of marriage.

Although friendship does not usually involve an explicit pact, a kind of pact does exist carrying with it obligations of fidelity: that the friends remain spiritually close, that they help and defend each other if necessary, that they speak well of each other, keep confidences, and so on.

Commitments between persons require that the parties give themselves. That may require sacrifice. There is no real friendship when only one party gives and only one receives. True friendship is not based on material interest, and hard times are an occasion for testing it, not terminating it.

Something similar is true in matrimony, a much more complex relationship which we shall consider in the next chapter.

Our closest neighbors are those bound to us by kinship—parents, children, siblings. They are the first ones to whom we should intend good and avoid harming. But that may not be easy. Knowing them so well, we may be tired of their ways, their talk, their ideas, their defects, so that we treat them worse than mere acquaintances. It is a fundamental moral principle that the special trials arising from closeness must be overcome.

This calls for constant effort—overlooking what's unpleasant, avoiding being a pest, eliminating small, cutting remarks, not thinking someone else is trying to annoy us on purpose. Such things can make life together unbearable and turn a relationship that should be a source of happiness into torment.

In their place, we need to forgive, ignore stupidities and small conflicts, always see a good intention behind what the other does, and forget small resentments instead of recalling them whenever provoked. If all the members of a family do that, family life is a blessing. And even if they don't, there is no better way. Sometimes we must supply the love others lack.

Love of God and Neighbor

Christianity teaches that all peoples are children of God. Therefore we must love everyone, nobody can be considered an enemy, and there is no right to ill-treat or be contemptuous of anybody. Even if someone considers himself our enemy, *we* cannot consider him ours.

The Lord says: "Love your enemies, do good to those who hate you. Bless those who curse you, pray for those who abuse you. . . . As you wish that men would do to you, do so to them. . . . Be merciful, even as your Father is merciful. Judge not and you will not be judged; condemn not, and you will not be condemned. Forgive and you will be forgiven; give, and it will be given to you; good measure, pressed down, shaken together, running over, will be put into your lap. For the measure you give, will be the measure you get back" (Lk 6:27–28).

God's logic is very different from man's. God seeks to conquer not with violence, but through the strength of love. St. John of the Cross wrote: "Put love where there is no love and you will bring forth love. This is the way of God." Critics consider it naïve to think this way, an invitation for others to take advantage of oneself. So it is. And so we need to change the way people think.

We have to learn to love *with God's love.* Christ asked this of his disciples when taking leave of them: "A new commandment I give to you, that you love one another: even as I have loved you, that you also love one another. By this all men will know that you are my disciples, if you have love for one another" (Jn 13:34–35).

One cannot separate love of God from love of neighbor. St. John says in his first letter: "He who does not love does not know God; for God is love" (1 Jn 4:8). And he adds: "God is love, and he who abides in love abides in God, and God abides in him. . . . If anyone says 'I love God', and hates his brother, he is a liar. For he who does not love his brother, whom he sees, cannot love God, whom he has not seen. And this commandment we have from him, that he who loves God should love his brother also" (1 Jn 4:16–21).

Human beings cannot love like this without God's help. Thus it is necessary to ask him humbly for such love, which throughout history has been a distinctive mark of true Christians. Yes, many Christians have not behaved like this and many do not now. But many have sacrificed their lives, virtually unnoticed, for love of neighbor. Millions of religious men and women have devoted themselves to caring for the sick, looking after abandoned children, giving shelter to the unwanted. Millions of ordinary Christians have spent themselves caring for old and infirm family members and the young, often under very hard conditions. Many in fact do love with the love of God. To experience it, it is necessary to live it.

There is an awesome text in Matthew's gospel in which the Lord speaks of the final judgment. Separating people one from another as a shepherd separates sheep from goats, with the sheep at his right hand and the goats at his left, he will say to those on the right, "Come, O blessed of my Father, inherit the kingdom prepared for you from the foundation of the world; for I was hungry and you gave me food, I was thirsty and you gave me drink, I was a stranger and you welcomed me, I was naked and you clothed me, I was sick and you visited me, I was in prison and you came to me."

These are precisely the works of mercy mentioned earlier. But the words of the Lord will surprise the just when they hear them: "Lord, when did we see thee hungry and feed thee, or thirsty and give thee drink? And when did we see thee a stranger and welcome thee, or naked and clothe thee? And when did we see thee sick or in prison and visit thee?" And the Lord will reply, "Truly, I say to you, as you did it to one of the least of these my brethren, you did it to me" (Mt 25:32–40).

8

The Transmission of Life

The Truth about Sex

Contrary to what some people imagine, sexuality is not the central issue in morality, although it is an important one. Nature itself tells us what its rules and laws are. The source of the confusion in this area is too much noise—too many arguments and claims making it impossible to think calmly.

In human beings, as in animals, the sexual instinct is strong, and there is a specific pleasure associated with it. That pleasure is a good. But it becomes bad when the order of goods and duties is not respected.

This, however, is not the big issue about sex. The central question is instead the natural function of sexuality. And the fact is that sex is ordered to *the transmission of life.* Sexuality has many other aspects, but this is fundamental.

The sexual organs of men and women are complementary and facilitate reproduction, which can occur naturally whether the partners intend it or not. Sexual attraction is a biological mechanism for the conservation of the species. And sexual pleasure is like an ornament that makes it more attractive. The good of pleasure is ordered to the good of the species.

But is it licit to separate these two things, transmission of life and sexual pleasure, which are united in nature? May one seek sexual pleasure without respecting the transmission of life? Would this be according to human dignity?

These questions become clearer if one takes as an analogy a function like digestion. In the most decadent period of the Roman Empire, wealthy people attended banquets at which exquisite dishes were served, ate their fill, and then provoked vomiting so that they could continue eating. The pleasure of eating was separated from its biological purpose, nutrition. Was this moral, that is, worthy of human dignity?

So repugnant is this practice that it can easily be seen to be a disorder. The separation of sex and reproduction is, however, no different in moral terms, and the fact that sexual pleasure is stronger than the pleasure of eating does not alter the moral reality.

It is immoral to procure sexual pleasure in ways other than conjugal relationships between a man and a woman, and it is immoral when the transmission of life is thwarted, either by drugs or by mechanical means.

The Sexual Taboo

On the basis of the biological truth of sex, let us now consider its social and human aspects.

Sex is not just one more biological function, but the way life is transmitted to new human beings. Thus it is easy to understand something implicit in all the great religions and cultures, something that Frank Sheed expressed wisely: "*Life must be sacred, sex must be sacred, marriage must be sacred.*" Since human life is sacred, so, too, are sex, the source of life, and matrimony, the place where this function takes place.

Religious respect toward sex, expressed in strict moral rules, has been called a taboo (in the original Polynesian meaning:

something set apart as sacred). This means it is something to be treated with great respect and needs particular attention.

Our culture has lost a great deal of its sensitivity in this area. Failing to understand the profound wisdom of the sexual taboo, it looks on it as a limitation of freedom rather than an important protection of the dignity of human life. Respect for sex has thus been lost. Its sacred character has disappeared, and it has been vulgarized, while the sacred character of marriage and the sanctity of human life also have been disappearing.

There is an urgent need to recover a deep vision of sexuality along with a proper regard for all the other great realities of life that are threatened by the consumer mentality: friendship, beauty, wisdom, serenity—values delicate and unseen but literally priceless. Morality, the art of living well, does not seek to repress sexuality, but to protect it and recognize its value.

Sexuality is the basis of the most important social institution, the family. Families are inextricably linked to the origin of new life and to the deep marital relationships that give rise to a home, the proper human environment for the growth and development of a new generation. By the same token, sexuality is an important element of full human happiness, since happiness is closely related to love, and the strongest human loves tend to originate in the family.

Sexuality also is an important part of the social order. The family is the normal environment where people grow up and learn to live as members of society.

Given the importance of sexuality, then, it is understandable that all well-ordered societies have treated it as something sacred and insisted on sexual discipline, including marriage laws, a minimum age for marriage, and other precautions. Lack of such discipline is a sign of decadence that weakens the central fibers of personal and social life by destroying families, impeding or preventing human development, causing economic problems, and loosing a host of destructive attitudes and forms of behavior that break down social order. All this is to say that lack of sexual discipline is a veritable Pandora's Box, the root cause of innumerable personal and social ills.

Sexual morality is a matter of respecting what nature has determined as the reality of sex. Here above all we do not have the option of creating a morality according to our taste. Instead we must discover and respect the pre-existing laws of nature. Our only chance is to live or not to live according to our condition—in a manner proper to human beings or not.

Sex and the Family

Masculinity and femininity are two different ways of being human, involving different sensibilities and ways of acting. One is not better than the other, but the differences are pervasive, since sexuality affects all levels of the person.

This basically is why the superficial and sporadic use of sexuality simply for the sake of pleasure, though producing an ephemeral satisfaction, is followed by frustration.

Sexuality is not just physiology, any more than being a man or a woman is just having sexual organs. The complementarity of sexual differences goes much further than that.

Perhaps without being aware of it, man seeks in woman what he does not have: kindness, tenderness, beauty, love for details, understanding. Woman seeks decisiveness, security, fortitude, shelter. It's not that women lack fortitude or men, tenderness, but there is a tenderness proper to women that men seek, and a fortitude proper to men that women appreciate.

This is reflected in the experience of falling in love. Sexual attraction, though real, is not the heart of romantic passion. Rather, falling in love involves the whole person. Intimacy is not just about sex but extends to the many feelings, ideas, desires, and aspirations a man and woman seek to share in an intimate relationship. This in turn creates a special friendship, somehow related to sexuality.

It is true that relationships between men and women tend to have some element of sexuality, but this need not be the case. There are many man-woman social relationships in which sex does not play a part and has no reason to.

Sexuality is, however, an element in the special friendship that sometimes develops between a woman and a man. Such friendship tends to be exclusive, resistant to being shared with another party. When a man and a woman fall in love and recognize this situation, a kind of covenant develops between them. Because the mutual feelings are exclusive, they cannot be shared with anybody else.

C.S. Lewis expresses it very well in his book *The Four Loves*. Exclusivity is not present in other kinds of friendship, and a normal person is happy when his friends are friends with one another. But a normal man or woman would consider it treasonous for the beloved to love someone else along with himself or herself. This jealousy is the response of one who feels deceived.

When sexuality is understood only as something physical whose goal is only the satisfaction of desire, the human relationship is unimportant and need not be exclusive. But when human sexuality is seen in all its richness, exclusivity is essential and personal intimacy is required.

When falling in love leads to marriage, a home is established and a family is born. Thus human sexuality is integrated into a rich, complex relationship between persons, and biological fertility is integrated into the natural institution of matrimony.

A man and a woman do not create the laws of marriage, any more than they do the laws of sexuality. They are doing something that belongs to human nature, whose laws they cannot change.

The intimate and exclusive relationship between spouses gives rise to mutual help and support. This spousal self-giving, reinforced by affective and passionate elements, is a school of humanity. When Jesus says in the gospel that husband and wife form *one flesh*, he is referring to a deep unity with both physical and spiritual aspects.

Sexual relations express, extend, and reinforce the friendship and mutual self-giving of spouses and help them understand and love each other. This same act that expresses and reinforces the love of spouses is nature's way of transmitting human life. Living sexuality well requires respecting this law. As Pope John Paul II says, *we cannot separate the unitive meaning* (the union of the spouses) *and the procreative meaning* (giving life).

This does not mean spouses intend the transmission of life; it is enough that the nature of the conjugal act be respected. But it is immoral to deform that act or use artificial means (condoms, spermicides, contraceptives, etc.) that render conception impossible or suppress it (abortifacient drugs).

Human sexuality in its fullness integrates these elements: conjugal union, exclusivity of sexual and affective self-giving, friendship and mutual gift, openness to the transmission of life and the upbringing of children.

Clearly, though, things aren't always ideal. Married life can and frequently does call for a sort of heroism, and this may be hard at times. But many and important goods of the person and of society depend on it.

Difficulties plainly do occur in marriage. Some spouses never do come to love each other or, after a time, stop loving each other. Marriages of convenience often end in failure (but some succeed). Some situations become insufferable. But none of this makes marriage cease to be what it is or alters the laws of sexuality and human happiness. It would be a hideous mistake to eradicate the idea of marriage because some marriages don't correspond to the ideal. That would be like denying the laws of vision because some people can't see. It makes far more sense to use all the social and personal means necessary for marriage to succeed.

Success in married life is far more important than professional or social success and requires effort. Society should help. If serious steps were taken to put into effect social measures to enhance the chances of matrimonial success, the problems we now see on all sides would be fewer and less grave.

And if a marriage fails? The union of a man and a woman in marriage is for life. There are bound to be some failures, but the norm does not change and it must be upheld and fostered. As for the difficult cases, they must be studied and resolved in the concrete. Meanwhile the best medicine for marital failure is the preventative kind.

Family Love

When Christian morality speaks of sex, it is speaking of the family. Sex finds its natural place in marriage, where it is the origin of new lives. Without this natural focus, sexuality loses its human meaning.

The family is the principal setting of human love, and is built on the basis of love: founded on the love of spouses, growing by their love and fidelity, realized by their love for their children, and reaching fulfillment when the children learn to love their parents, each other, and everybody else.

To be sure, a family is not a utopia. True love grows in the ordinary circumstances of life, amid daily work, discomfort, health problems, economic worries, fatigue, and outbursts of anger.

While it produces feelings, and to a degree originates in feelings, it is not itself a feeling. *Marital love should not be confused with the transitory experience of "falling in love."*

With the passing of time, the positive and negative qualities of the other become apparent. Then, if there is confidence, intimacy grows, and that first falling in love gives way to affection and real love.

Affection grows as the couple live more of their life in common. But to share, one must give. Love always means self-giving, losing something for the benefit of the other.

This may require sacrifice—doing things one doesn't like, not doing what one does like, adjusting one's desires, giving more thought to the satisfaction of the other than to one's own. But it is only on the basis of sacrifice that love lasts. This means learning to overlook defects, repeatedly forgive, avoid grudges, ignore angry outbursts, impatience, and unpleasant remarks. Otherwise problems are magnified, misunderstandings grow, and life together becomes intolerable.

It is a characteristic of love to go to excess. If both parties are sticklers for rights and duties, and no more, the marriage has already failed to some extent. People can't live that way. One day he's tired, next day she's on edge—and insisting on one's rights in such situations is a formula for constant warfare. Love is only possible when both parties are prepared to do more than justice requires and at least one of them is willing to sacrifice.

The greatest human happiness on earth consists precisely in love—not so much being loved, as loving. A person who loves feels happy, even if love is unrequited, though in that case happiness and pain are mixed.

Love is not to be confused with sentimentality, however, or with affective passion. True love seeks first and foremost the happiness of the loved one, while sentimental and passionate loves are possessive and can be expressions of selfishness.

Marriage lived well is a great school of humanity because it is a great school of love. Sacrificing for the other provides the warmth of a home. And that makes a home a good place to receive new lives.

Great sacrifices are necessary to support a child. Parents unaccustomed to sacrifices will be unable to raise their children properly. Moreover, as the place where the precept to love one's neighbor as oneself takes root, the family is a great school of social life. To understand sexual morality one must know what a family is.

9

The Roots of Humanity

A Being with Roots

If the world were as it should be, everyone would be born into a home, a loving place where he or she would be accepted and cared for. But for whatever reason or reasons, many are born without homes. That does not make them less worthy than others, but it is a lack, a loss, with whose consequences society must cope.

Human infants require much attention—physical (babies must be fed and protected from harm) and also spiritual (they must be taught to live in a human way, including behaving toward others as a human should). They must be taught how to talk and helped to understand the world around them. Small children inspire strong natural feelings of tenderness among normal adults, especially their mothers.

The first lessons leave a deep mark on a person. Strong bonds develop with people and things. Normally the child will love his parents and those who care for him, and will become quite dependent on them. Strong bonds are also created with the environment—rooms, places, landscapes, smells, foods, customs. All these experiences help to shape a person's lifelong identity.

For a human being, these early bonds to persons and things are like roots for a tree: they feed him, make him grow, situate him in the world. Rootless people, not bound by affection to places or persons, are in a certain way inhuman, lacking depth or definition.

Bonding to a family grafts one into the history of a human group and into a cultural tradition with origins. These invisible ties are much stronger, more complex, and more extensive than might at first be thought. Those who live today inhabit a world shaped and improved by those who came before.

Education brings ways of thinking and behaving, customs and social usages, habits, working techniques—a *spiritual patrimony* that makes one part of a human tradition. Yet people are largely oblivious to the fact that the existing social order and what it provides are results of much work and time. They suppose everything has always been as it is, even though something as apparently simple as a traffic light represents a great human accomplishment.

Maturity and the Common Good

We have a moral duty to appreciate what we have received. This is called gratitude.

Usually, we can't give back as much as we've been given. No matter how well we treat our parents, we can never fully repay them. The same is true, though to a lesser degree, of those who've contributed to our education, and indeed of very many others. A multitude of material and immaterial goods come to us thanks to the efforts of people throughout history. We can only be thankful.

The first step in that is to acknowledge and appreciate what we've received. Since we cannot pay back those responsible, thankfulness must take the form of helping those who come after us as we've been helped.

Maturity lies in transcending the childish mentality that looks always to receive, recognizing our responsibilities, and providing for those who will follow us and those now in need—the old, children, the sick. This is clear in small societies where everyone knows everyone else but harder to grasp in more complex societies. Someone living in a big city may not even notice that he or she isn't caring for others. But this is an empty way of life. Happiness requires relating to others, giving oneself to them, and contributing to the common good. No one can excuse himself from serving the society in which he lives.

The common good of a society is the huge collection of material and spiritual goods that make up its patrimony. A nation's common good includes, for example, its geography and landscapes, natural resources, customs and ways of life, productive capacity and infrastructures, educational and health systems, art, history, language, literature, and folklore. Less apparent, but also very important, are organization and education, public order, the efficiency and honesty of institutions, public morality, its cultural level, and so on.

The common good requires that these goods be well distributed—that all members of the society participate in them: for example, by the wide distribution of private property, access to education and culture, equal opportunity to work and take part in public life. And each responsible member of the society has a serious obligation toward its common good, with duties that arise naturally and do not depend on personal opinions or politics. Moreover, those who can do so must contribute more to the common good than they receive since there will always be those who cannot contribute their share: children, the poor, the sick.

Doing one's job well is the usual way of contributing to the common good, since all honest work fosters the development and order of society. People also contribute by caring for those who depend on them: family, friends, subordinates.

The common good also is served by protecting or increasing material and spiritual goods that comprise it. This may be done by individuals or groups, including voluntary associations.

The Role of Authority

Left to themselves to decide how to contribute to the common good, many people would settle for what was easy and neglect what was hard. The regulation of individual initiatives may therefore be necessary. That is the role of public authority, which must care for the common good and regulate the contribution of all, distributing tasks and benefits, and creating stable conditions. It may involve asking more of those with more to give and less from those with less. Decisions should be made justly, according to legitimate laws and with clear, truthful explanations.

The authority of government must be respected. St. Paul in his epistles asks for prayers for the emperor—Nero, a tyrant who in the end beheaded Paul. Honest and constructive criticism of authorities is in order, but the function of authority itself must not be undermined.

Ideally, all members of society would obey the law willingly, but some will always disobey, and authorities must be able to punish them, particularly in matters of a criminal nature.

Nevertheless, authority is limited. Government does not own society and cannot do whatever it wants. The authority should limit itself by reasonable criteria of justice, while explaining laws to the public as much as possible and refraining from merely arbitrary actions.

Social order requires respect for the laws, norms, and customs of society. Manifestly unjust laws may be disobeyed, but this right should be exercised very carefully, and it is prudent to consult first with someone skilled at moral analysis.

The Principle of Subsidiarity

Government and society are not identical, and government should not control all social activities. Abuses in governing often reflect a fundamental lack of confidence in the people, along with the idea that the governing class is the privileged elite. The result very often is that rulers come to think of themselves as exempt from rules that apply to others.

There are no magical ways of making a society honest. Law alone is not enough. First it is necessary to know what it is to be good. To a great extent, that is the role of education.

But getting people to *want* to be good is more difficult. That is the work of conscience. Government can help only from the outside, rewarding good and punishing evil, and promoting a just social order.

While government should foster the common good, it cannot do that alone but should encourage and guide social activity that serves the common good. Christian social morality proposes subsidiarity as a principle useful to this end.

The *principle of subsidiarity* could be formulated as "problems should be tackled at the lowest level at which they can be dealt with effectively." Thus, the family is the preferred setting for raising children, and education should be under local control as much as possible. Needs ordinarily are better known at the lower level, and solutions tend to be more effective. National government should handle only those problems too large to be solved locally or by individuals; its role otherwise is to help the local initiatives.

In the end, there are no perfect solutions for the problems of society. A prudent solution will be based on human dignity and respect for society's members. All have a right and duty to contribute intelligently to the common good.

10

With All the Strength of the Soul

Because God Exists

"Thou shalt love the Lord thy God with thy whole heart, and with thy whole soul, and with thy whole mind, and with thy whole strength." As we have seen, this is the first and most important commandment. God is not just one more thing. He is the most important being, on whom everything else depends. We must love him "more than all things" simply because he is above all. Morality observes this order of reality.

But it is impossible to love God above all things if one doesn't believe he exists, and his existence is more or less frequently questioned today. For nearly all peoples and cultures of previous times, however, God's existence was obvious. People found the signs of God's presence and action all around them.

To a degree, our world has become desacralized. Many people think everything is matter, even themselves, and this materialistic prejudice makes it hard for them to find God. The problem is with the prejudice, not God.

Thomas Aquinas says God is present where he acts, and so is present in all things inasmuch as he creates them and sustains them in existence. Thus we can see God's action in nature—in landscapes and the heavens, in deserts and forests, lightning and storms. All offer a glimpse of God's hand.

Above all else, however, *God is found within the human spirit.* We will not find him elsewhere unless we find him there. Scripture calls this interior nucleus of the human person "the heart." Here one finds the person's conscience and his loves.

Here, too, is where we find God within us, by a presence "more intimate to me than myself," as St. Augustine says. In finding God in landscapes and storms, one is finding an exterior reflection of what we carry within us.

Still, it is possible to see nature only as matter. If our vision is too materialistic, it is difficult to see beauty and even more difficult to see God. To do that, we need to look behind the multiplicity of phenomena, go beyond the material and physical.

To say "behind" or "beyond" is of course figurative language. God is not above or below. Similarly, the positive sciences have their own way of looking at things, "dissecting" them as it were, and then concluding that everything is no more than the sum of its measurable, quantifiable parts. While this materialistic vision can be useful in many ways, it can also be a hindrance preventing one from seeing a whole that can't be reduced to its parts (the beauty of a landscape, the vision of a poem). The thrust of materialism is toward the destruction of beauty.

So, too, with human dignity, justice, truth, friendship, love, and many other deep human realities. They exist in a different way, on a different plane, than stones.

Think of the universe as a kind of pyramid. Matter is its base. But the pyramid has many levels, and whoever believes in God knows he is at the apex. God gives full meaning to the world of beauty, of truth, of love—to the whole universe of meaningful things.

Unavoidably, one who does not believe in God sees a flat world. Those who do not succumb to materialistic reductionism may believe in realities that the spirit grasps—beauty, truth—and so raise the pyramid a level or two. But unless God is at the apex, the pyramid is truncated and incoherent. With God at the apex, however, everything falls into place. This, the order of reality, is also the foundation of the moral order, the order of loves.

God and the Voice of Conscience

God is not our equal or our partner. He is our creator and gives us our being. Our relationship with him is therefore totally different from other relationships.

Moreover, revelation tells us we are made to love God. The commandment to love God above all else is not an external imposition but the most intimate and fundamental law of our being. We cannot be happy in any other way. St. Augustine says: "Lord, you made us for you, and our heart is restless until it rests in you."

Thus, whether one knows it or not, the history of one's life is in its deepest sense the history of one's relationship with him. The success of a man or woman's life lies in coming to love God above everything.

Since, however, no one can be forced to love anything, fulfilling the commandment to love God above everything does not come from forcing oneself to love him, but from encountering him and interacting with him. This does not happen all at once. It is a process. The best human loves can give us some idea of it.

It involves more than thinking about loving God, and includes learning how he wants to be loved. This takes place in the intimacy of conscience.

Someone faithful to his or her conscience grasps that *conscience is an echo of God's voice.* To obey conscience is, in the end, to obey him, while rejecting conscience is rejecting him, inasmuch as he is the foundation of the moral order that conscience discovers.

Moral life is a relationship with God. Nothing, no matter how small, lies outside its scope; each of our free decisions is made in his presence. Morality is a lifestyle based on the relationship with God, the art of growing in love for him.

Here is what distinguishes morality from ethics. Ethics is a product of philosophical analysis that identifies principles to be considered in acting. Ethical man tries to be faithful to these principles, while moral man tries to be faithful to God.

Yet there are not two moralities, and it would be absurd to consider oneself above the commandments—the moral norms—that God has revealed and the ethical principles discovered by right reason. On the contrary, morality embraces all true human ethics. The conscience of someone who has received a good moral formation and tries to live correctly will move spontaneously within that framework, not seeing it as a limitation but as an aid.

Within that framework, God has left ample room for human freedom. Moral norms indicate what ought not to be done and provide an order of values and goals of behavior that flesh out the commandments to love God and neighbor. Great room remains for creativity in realizing goods.

Another saying of St. Augustine is relevant here: "Love and then do as you will." The highest principle of behavior, in which all morality is summed up, is love. But this must be understood correctly. Augustine doesn't say "Do as you will and then love" but, "Love and then do as you will." One who truly loves God above all things will always do what God wants. Guided by the love of God, conscience learns to set our loves in proper order.

Veneration and Offense

In carrying out what God asks of us in our consciences, we come to love him more and more easily discover what he wants. Only in drawing near to him do we grasp what it means for him to be God. Yet in the outside world, God remains hidden. Nature, Blessed John Henry Cardinal Newman remarked, is ambiguous, both revealing and at the same time hiding, the Creator. Only in the depths of the human heart can one intuit him.

This may be the deepest mystery of all. *We are made for God, yet he does not simply appear to us—we need to seek him.* He wants our love, but he does not force it. If we seek him we will find him, but otherwise we will not.

From a distance, God seems hidden. Only as we approach him do we begin to comprehend what great veneration and love he deserves. God becomes known to us insofar as we love him.

The great respect owed God extends to everything connected with him: worship, sacred vessels, persons and places dedicated to his worship. Holy Scripture sometimes calls this veneration "holy fear of the Lord." It is part of observing the first three commandments of the Decalogue.

Getting close to God involves discovering the infinite contrast between his greatness and our nothingness. Every authentic encounter with God brings with it a fresh realization of our own weakness and the many gifts we have received from him. This recognition of the deepest truth of our condition leads to true humility, confident petition, and thanksgiving.

As we approach him, we also come to see another unsuspected reality: the mystery of sin. Our guilty failures and weaknesses are not just superficial mistakes but truly offenses against God, refusals of what he asks of us.

Here is another clear difference between morality and ethics. The ethical man regrets his mistakes and, if he is an upright person, tries to avoid them in the future. But Christians know they need to ask forgiveness from God, as from a friend one has offended, and must do something out of the ordinary to show that, despite everything, their love is true.

Moreover, the recognition of sin increases as we progress morally. Paradoxically, those closer to God have a greater perception of sin than those far away.

People with an underdeveloped moral life have a weak sense of sin. Indeed, to them the very notion of sin seems alien and absurd. If they have some degree of moral sensitivity, they understand sin to be a transgression of a moral norm and may grasp that it is an offense against God, but that makes little impression on them. Only as the moral life develops does one come to regard rejection of God as sin's most important aspect. Then one feels the need to show real repentance, to compensate in some way.

Repenting is not a matter of feeling pain. It is more a decision—a determination to ask pardon and renew the friendship that has suffered injury. Feeling may or may not be present. This is how it is in our dealings with God.

The Commitment of Love

God is not an idea, a principle, or a norm. Relationships with him are person to person commitments. These personal bonds generate duties of loyalty.

The Gospels of St. Mark, St. Matthew, and St. Luke all tell of an incident that sheds light on this. In chapter 10 of St. Mark we read of a young man who approaches Jesus and asks, "What must I do to inherit eternal life?" Jesus answers, "You know the commandments." The young man says, "Teacher, all these I have observed from my youth." At that, Jesus looks lovingly upon him and tells him, "You lack one thing; go, sell what you have, and give to the poor, and you will have treasure in heaven; and come, follow me." But then, the gospel recounts, "his countenance fell, and he went away sorrowful, for he had great possessions."

This young man had lived close to God, and that led him to the verge of a greater commitment. It always happens like that:

God calls those who draw near him. Choosing to be weak in the world, he chooses also to find support in the weakness of those who love him.

Commitment arises from knowing and loving God—and great commitment from knowing and loving him greatly. Nothing is more beautiful or the source of more joy. And this love is compatible with everything truly human, since all goods are ordered to God.Though easy to understand in theory, trying to live this way requires courage. When the young man went away sad, Jesus said to his disciples, "How hard it will be for those who trust in riches to enter the kingdom of God. . . . It is easier for a camel to go through the eye of a needle than for a rich man to enter the kingdom of God."

Here are hard words meant to warn the disciples that it is easy to lose one's way. Although the young man had lived a good life, at the most important moment of his existence, when God offered him his friendship, he preferred worldly wealth.

"Then who can be saved?" the disciples exclaimed. To which Jesus replied, "With men it is impossible, but not with God." Nothing is impossible for God, including empowering us to love him above all things.

God has called us from the moment he willed our existence and has sought us ever since. All of a person's life is a growing response to or rejection of that call. Thus *the success or failure of the moral life can be measured by one's love of God.*

One may enter into a relationship with God hoping to get some benefit from it, but if one perseveres, the main benefit is to give witness to God's love. This friendship makes demands on all aspects of our being and acting. As in a good human friendship, each party continually demands more from the other.

But it is a loving demand, made with recognition of the fact that improvement takes time and effort and is an ongoing project pursued with the help, understanding, and patience of the other.

Love always ennobles, and this can be seen in the most material and most spiritual details. Someone in love does many things he or she would otherwise not do because the beloved wishes them done. Clearly this is how it is in a successful marriage. And it is like that also in the relationship with God. God wants us to improve, and our desire to do so becomes felt as a need.

Every love has a history. Born at a given moment, it either grows or dies, matures or withers. It is life's greatest treasure, which alone gives authentic happiness. This is why the whole of morality is concerned with building up love of God and neighbor, with the best of all loves, the love of God.

The love of God passes through different stages, described by mystics like St. Teresa of Avila and St. John of the Cross. They compare it with climbing a mountain, an image with a long tradition that was already familiar to early Christians.

The first stage is discovery, falling in love. This produces enthusiasm, which God uses to propose his first demands to eliminate things like sloth, selfishness, and sensuality that hamper or distort love of God. Conscience begins to recognize them and demands their removal.

As time passes, the novelty goes, the initial enthusiasm fades, and one becomes more aware of the struggle entailed in ridding oneself of defects. The experience of failure teaches that climbing this mountain won't be as easy or quick as one imagined. The impulse to persist comes now from fidelity to the love of God and the claims of conscience.

Progress is not measured by likes and dislikes, since these embody much egoism. God makes use of life's difficulties and sufferings to perfect one who loves him. He purifies love by removing gratification and permitting sorrows. Usually these are not momentous but relatively trivial—small health problems, job setbacks, problems in human relationships. We must accept them without too much complaining—or, better, with no complaining at all.

Acquiring a more mature love, fed by better knowledge of God and more intense contact with him, requires that one spend time in *mental prayer.* Prayer is the foundation of the spiritual life. There is no seeking or understanding God without the habit of mental prayer. To grasp God's logic, one must meditate on what is happening, examine one's life, ask for light. Perseverance in mental prayer requires devoting a fixed time to it.

The ascent of the mountain will now proceed with a joy that is deeper, though less obvious, than the enthusiasm of the beginning. There may be periods of darkness, pain, or misunderstanding. These are part of what St. John of the Cross called "the dark night of the soul." But God does not abandon anyone who does not abandon him. Mystics, like St. Gregory of Nyssa, St. Teresa, and St. John have traced the stages of this ascent, and someone who wishes to know more should consult their work. There is a beautiful summary of the itinerary in St. Josemaría Escrivá's homily *Towards Holiness.*[1]

All this constitutes a precious and hidden knowledge, discovered and understood only by those brave enough to make the ascent. To others it seems crazy, absurd. But this is the way that leads to God and his love. One begins by looking for him within one's soul.

1. *Friends of God* (New York: Scepter Publishers, 1981), nos. 294–316.

PART III

GRACE

Up to this point, we have looked at the foundation of morality (goods and duties, conscience and freedom), and reviewed our duties toward other realities (the material world, other people, society, God). We have made use mainly of what can be discovered by reason, only rarely turning to Christian doctrine to buttress a point or borrow a particularly apt expression. Everything else was accessible to nonbelievers as well as believers, and in fact many people of good will do share these views.

In the last chapter, however, the approach changed. There we reached the religious level, the proper level of morality. We acknowledged the need to deal personally with God, the value of conscience as God's voice, sin as an offense to God and repentance as reconciliation with him, and the moral life as personal commitment to God.

All this is part of Christian morality, but not what is proper to it. *The essential element in Christian morality is Christ.* Beyond studying ethical principles that reason can discover and religious motivations that supply strength and meaning to our conduct, we must speak of the mysteries of the life of Christ and consider why Christ is the center of Christian morality.

In this third part of the book, therefore, we shall deal with the mystery of his life and death, of the mystical insertion of each Christian into his life, and the vital manifestations of union with Christ. In the end, we shall see that Christian morality can be called "the art of living in Christ."

11

The Christian Mystery

Christ's Anointing

When the Lord asked the apostles what people were saying about him and Peter replied, it turned out that what people thought then was very much like what they think now: some believed Jesus was a prophet, a man of God. Others saw him as a teacher of great moral wisdom. Others thought he was crazy or an impostor (Peter did not mention them). Then the Lord asked, "But who do you say that I am?"

Peter's response mirrors perfectly the faith of the Church: "Thou art the Christ, the Son of the living God." Christ is a Greek word with the same meaning as Messiah in Hebrew: "anointed." When we speak the name Jesus Christ, we make a confession of faith: Jesus of Nazareth is the Christ, the Messiah of God, awaited by Israel.

Seeing what that means would take us very deeply into the history and mentality of Israel. For now it is enough to know that the Messiah was someone longed for in whom all God's promises to Israel would be fulfilled.

But why "anointed"? Because in Israel, as in other cultures, men destined for important missions were consecrated and anointed with a special oil as a sign of their selection by God as well as a guarantee that God would empower them to do what they were called to do. Kings, priests, and prophets were anointed and consecrated.

The Messiah, however, was not to be simply one more in this line but the one anointed with the Spirit of God. He would have all the strength and energy of God.

The mystery of Christ, anointed by the Spirit of God, is revealed throughout his life. In words and deeds, Jesus of Nazareth shows that he is truly the Son of God, participates fully and eternally in the divine intimacy, and is therefore filled with the Spirit of God, the Holy Spirit.

The mystery of Christ is expressed in the symbolism of a beautiful episode found in all four gospels, the baptism of the Lord.

As John the Baptist was baptizing at the Jordan River, Jesus came and asked to be baptized. John refused, feeling unworthy, but Jesus insisted. At that moment, a voice was heard saying, "This is my beloved Son, in whom I am well pleased." A dove hovered over Jesus, and John understood that the mystery of the Messiah was being revealed to him, since the dove represented the Holy Spirit.

The Church understands that Jesus of Nazareth fulfills the promises of covenant, salvation, and plenitude made by God to Israel, and that Jesus is the true Son of God—as the Creed says, "eternally begotten of the Father, God from God, Light from Light, true God from true God."

In the mystery of Christ, morality takes on an entirely new dimension. God has become man so that we can participate in divine life. In Scripture, the symbolic name of the Messiah is Emmanuel, "God is with us." God wanted to live among us, not just two thousand years ago in Israel but in the life of each Christian now. The heart of Christian life is identifying with Christ, living in him, with him, and for him.

Each Christian, too, is anointed by the Holy Spirit and made a child of God. Each is called to fulfillment in the person of Christ and to participation in his salvific mission.

Christ's death and resurrection reveal what sin is and provide the means to vanquish it. Through his death and resurrection, God gives us the opportunity to atone for our sins and become his children. This is Christian morality.

Sin and the Cross

Accustomed as we are to the cross as the chief symbol of Christianity, we are likely to overlook it. It stands atop churches, hangs on our walls or on our breasts, and hardly seems horrible or disconcerting. But the cross represents a dreadful paradox: the Son of God became man and was crucified.

"He came unto his own," says St. John, "and his own received him not." Not only didn't they receive him, but they persecuted him and finally killed him. We should not take this for granted. God became man because he wanted to live among his people, sharing our joys and sorrows, and he was brutally rejected and sent to the cross.

This was done, moreover, by the leaders of the people of Israel, the people elected by God, with whom he had established a covenant. The nation that expected a Messiah rejected him because he did not fit their idea.

This terrible mistake—this terrible sin—happened only once in history. But it should not be thought that this horrible rejection of God involved only the Lord's contemporaries. We are all implicated in the mystery of that terrible injustice.

Those who killed Jesus did not know he was God. They believed he was a particularly bothersome man. Had they known he was the Son of God, they would not have dared do as they did. But to sin one need not intend to kill God. Indeed, human beings do not have a capacity for evil like that.

Yet how would we treat God if he were truly within our reach? In Christ, he was. And we very likely would have done as men did then: persecuting him or approving of his persecution—or just running away out of fear.

Think how we behave now. God is here, though we may not recognize him, and we persecute, reject, and abandon him. Often we flee from the God who speaks in our consciences. It is no great trick for us to mistreat this God within us.

God is not just in the depths of one's conscience, though. He is also in the people we encounter. Recall the Lord's words about the final judgment: "Depart from me, you cursed. . . . I was hungry, and you gave me no food, I was thirsty and you gave me no drink." And those are only the omissions. Suppose we have insulted, humiliated, deceived, and abused others.

Not all sins are equal, nor did all those who took part in the killing of Christ do so in the same way. Some abandoned him out of fear, some were indifferent, some persecuted him in rage. We also sin in these ways.

Outright hatred of God is no doubt difficult. But even though, not seeing God, we don't hate him, we can hate the manifestations of his grace.

That often happens in settings like offices, factories, barracks, or dormitories where there is a truly good person, honest and just, who fulfills duties, treats others with affection, and is always good tempered. Some will admire this individual, without feeling capable of imitating him. Some will pity him because they consider him naïve. And some will be annoyed at his presence just because he's good. Their reactions are likely to range from slightly cutting jokes to deeds that express a genuinely pathological hatred.

The presence of goodness angers people because it makes them face their own deviant behavior. Up to now they may have been able to silence conscience, but the presence of a good person is an unspoken reproach to their unrepented evil.

This is why all upright men and women suffer persecution sooner or later. Christ predicted it, as we read in the Gospel of St. John: "If the world hates you, know that it has hated me before you. If you were of the world, the world would love its own. But because you are not of the world, but I chose you out of the world, therefore the world hates you. Remember the word that I said to you: A servant is not greater than his master. If they persecuted me, they will persecute you" (Jn 15:18–20).

All of us are implicated in the death of Christ, because all participate in the rejection of God. And so we all contribute to poisoning the world, harming ourselves, our families, and our society.

The Meaning of Suffering

Pain has a role in human maturing. We grow through the experience of difficulties and sorrows. There is no great achievement apart from great sacrifice. People who are given everything don't know how to sacrifice for an ideal, and they remain immature.

But there is a limit to this. Some sufferings destroy the spirit. There is the constructive pain of an athlete in training and the destructive pain that may accompany disease, the fear of death, discouragement and professional failure, economic collapse, the failure of projects, the anguish of seeing a loved one suffer, the triumph of injustice, the humiliation of the weak. Confronted with the problem of pain, we may demand an explanation from God. But until the end of time, the Cross is the only answer we will get.

The Son of God chose to become man and experience even the most arduous consequences of the human condition. God understands us. He is close to us. He shares our physical and moral pain, he knows what it is like to suffer, be despised, and die.

Thus *the Cross is also the symbol of God's solidarity with all who suffer,* especially the innocent. All human sufferings share in the mystery of the Cross, and all who suffer are somehow like other Christs. Apart from the mystery of the Cross, there is no comprehending the meaning of pain.

Christ accepts his suffering and turns it into prayer and sacrifice. He asks the Father to pardon human sins. With all else taken from him, he offers himself, the pain of his body, the anguish of his soul, and his death.

Since then, human suffering, united to the suffering of Christ, can be offered to God in testimony of love for him and for all men. Joined to Christ's suffering, it contributes to peace in the world, the triumph of justice, and the conversion of humankind.

That doesn't mean we should be indifferent to pain, suffering, injustice, and death. We resist these things and avoid them when possible. Yet very often that can't be done. Then, remembering Christ, we must accept them with love, unite ourselves to the Cross, and await resurrection with Christ.

Left to themselves, human beings would have looked for some other way of dealing with sin—for instance, violence, the punishment and destruction of sinners. But we don't think as God does. God preferred the Cross, and it is through the Cross, not force, that he seeks to convert the world.

St. Luke's gospel includes the precious account of the conversion of one of the criminals hanging on a cross next to Jesus. Seeing him suffering unjustly, the man repents and begs to be remembered in Christ's kingdom. The Lord forgives him at once and promises him eternal life. Here is a whole lesson on the Christian way of repairing the world.

The Paschal Mystery

It is a Utopian error to think we can solve the world's problems by human means alone. Evil's deepest cause is not a technical failure but a moral problem, sin, and the resulting separation from God. Here is the source of disorder in the human person, families, society, and the reason why it will not do to attempt to solve the problem with theoretical or technical solutions.

Ideological solutions to world problems have at times produced nightmare consequences. Think of the hellish Utopias of Nazism and Communism. It is the repeated folly of Utopias to ignore the problem of sin. Attributing all evils to something like private property or ignorance or somebody like the Jews or the bourgeoisie, they have forgotten that evil's cause is buried deep in the human heart.

Nor has technical progress been able to repair the world. True, it has helped people in some countries escape miserable living conditions and live dignified lives. Yet in many instances technical advances also have contributed to dehumanization and enslavement.

While continuing to use intelligence in seeking solutions to world problems, then, we must not forget that *the moral root of evil in the world is sin—separation from God.* Jesus makes this point clearly and forcefully (see Mt 15:19). And only God can heal human hearts in their depths, sometimes employing means we do not grasp.

Faced with evil in the world and in ourselves, we may cry out to God to do something. But God rarely intervenes as we would do. He allows history to follow its course, without either punishing evil or rewarding good actions at once. The just and the unjust succeed and fail, suffer and die, equally.

There is no such thing as perfect, complete justice in this life. Good is not fully recognized and rewarded, nor evil corrected and punished. Although we must do all we can so that the good will triumph in our hearts and in our deeds, we must accept the fact that God acts at a different level and we shall not understand his reasons until the end. Meanwhile, as in the Lord's parable, wheat and tares grow together in the world and in human hearts.

So God waits, as he does on the cross, the place where injustice has placed him. When we feel inclined to demand justice from God, let us remember that the crucifixion of this man who is God is the greatest injustice in all history, as well as God's chosen means of solving the problem of evil in the world. From the Cross, God works mysteriously and patiently in human hearts, converting them and bringing them close to him, strengthening those who allow him to speak in their consciences. God acts in the world by shaping the moral tenor of society through the free choices of individuals.

History began when the world came from God's hands and it will end when he takes it back. With us, the end of history is death. But in and through God it ends in Resurrection. Christ's resurrection means that the world's evil, sin, and injustice have been vanquished. The greatest injustice in history, our killing of the Son of God, has been righted. And resurrection now awaits all who unite themselves to the Cross and seek to live like Christ.

Still, just as Christ crossed over the threshold of death, so must we. All things must pass through the Cross and die in order to be restored. Our hearts must be purified, made capable of loving God above everything else, so that we can enter into his presence.

Suffering purifies; especially death, the great purifier of human pride.

When Christ returns in glory at the end of time, the process that began with his resurrection will be completed. The whole of history will be judged, and everything material and spiritual will be cleansed of sin's consequences. Human beings will rise, the just to share God's eternal life, the unjust to suffer eternal death. The good done in this life will enter purified into eternal life.

Christ's death and resurrection are the paschal mystery. *Pasch* means "passing," and in this, the most important Jewish feast, Israel recalled the "passing" from slavery in Egypt to become a nation, establish a covenant with God, and enter the Promised Land. The Christian Pasch celebrates the resurrection of Christ and all it signifies—our passing from the slavery of sin to life in Christ, our New Covenant with God, and the promise of eternal life.

12

The Body of Christ

Uniting Oneself to Christ

St. John's account of Christ's Last Supper discourse to the apostles contains a mysterious allegory: "I am the vine, you are the branches. He who abides in me, and I in him, he it is that bears much fruit; for apart from me you can do nothing" (Jn 15). The Lord is saying that his followers must join themselves to him and participate in his life.

Here is a great truth. Unless grafted into Christ like branches grafted into a vine, we will feel no impulse to live like Christ and have no strength to do so. Only united to him can we understand and live the ideals of the Christian life.

Christ's life comes to us through the action of the Holy Spirit, which transforms us, separating us from sin and turning us into sons and daughters of God. *The Spirit's action in the soul unites us to the mystery of Christ's life, death, and resurrection.*

This process of becoming joined to Christ has certain special moments, the sacraments. They symbolize and at the same time affect that union.

There are seven sacraments. Three especially recall the person and mission of Christ: baptism, confirmation, and the anointing of the sick. Two express and realize the unity of the Body of Christ, the Church: the Eucharist and penance. And two empower those who receive them for particular functions within this body: holy orders and matrimony. In the last section of the chapter we shall reflect on the relationship between the mysteries of Christ and ourselves.

Baptism has a twofold significance. One part of it is cleansing from sin. The other, recalling especially the baptism of Christ, is the anointing with the Holy Spirit by which the Christian becomes a child of God.

Church tradition surrounds baptism with several beautiful and expressive rites, of which the washing is central. It is washing not only with water but with the Holy Spirit.

St. Paul in the letter to the Romans (chapter 5) speaks of a new birth: the one who is baptized dies to sin and receives the life of Christ. This suggests the moral task of a Christian: with the help of the Holy Spirit, to let the consequences of sin die while striving to make his life reflect ever more perfectly the life of Christ.

The death of the old man and resurrection of the new, Christ, prepare the final resurrection. The Christian's transformation in Christ includes participation in Christ's resurrection. Death does not disappear, but by baptism it becomes a purifying path to eternal life. When a Christian is baptized, he begins to participate in that life and receives a pledge of the resurrection.

Union with the Holy Spirit, received at baptism, is confirmed in the sacrament called *confirmation.* The imposition of the hands of the bishop or his delegate and the anointing with specially consecrated oil confer a special seal, a confirmation in the Holy Spirit, to help one participate in Christ's mission. Faith is fortified and one receives strength to announce God's salvation.

This confirmation in the faith and mission of Christ first took place in a spectacular way on the Feast of Pentecost, fifty days after the resurrection of the Lord.

Until then, Christ's followers, not daring to manifest their faith publicly, had hidden out of fear. The action of the Holy Spirit filled them with zeal to announce Christ's message.

Ever since, the Church has known itself to be assisted by the Holy Spirit. Thanks to that help, she has preserved and interpreted Jesus' message down through the centuries, confident the Spirit will not allow it to be lost or contaminated by error and able to live it authentically and announce it with vigor.

In confirmation, the strength and courage conferred upon the primitive Church are conferred also upon each Christian. This makes it the sacrament of Christian maturity, when we should accept our own share of responsibility for the Church's work of living the life of Christ fully and communicating his message to all people.

The *anointing of the sick* is the sacrament administered to those suffering from a grave illness that places them in more or less proximate danger of death and to seniors aware that the moment of meeting the Lord definitively is close at hand. The priest anoints the person with consecrated oil and prays for him or her.

In early times, oil was used to treat wounds, and that is part of the symbolism of the sacrament. The Church asks God to cure the sick or give them strength to undergo sickness and death in a Christian fashion.

The sacrament also commemorates the mission of the Messiah, fulfilled on the Cross, as well as Christ's anointing by friendly hands at Bethany before his Passion and death. The sick person receives help to have the same disposition as Christ in the Garden of Olives: "Father, if it is possible, let this cup pass away from me; yet not as I will, but as thou willest." In a way, he or she becomes a priest, offering his or her own sacrifice to the Father in union with Christ. And at the moment of death, the Christian finds in this sacrament the consolation of such union.

Communion with Christ

The Church founded by Jesus Christ is a mystery of communion. It is not just a human society, a group of disciples more or less organized, but a communion in the Holy Spirit. The deepest bond of its communion is the Spirit, who therefore is said to be the Church's "soul."

St. Paul calls the Church the Body of Christ. It's "head" is Christ himself. Christians are united in Christ and among themselves by the Holy Spirit whom they carry in their souls, as well as by other bonds joining them to the visible institution that is the Church.

The Spirit animates the body of the Church and moves it to continue Christ's mission. With that assistance, the Church preaches Jesus' words and proclaims to the world the mystery of his death and resurrection.

Two sacraments, Eucharist and penance, refer directly to the Church. We shall consider them next. Then we shall turn to two sacraments related to the organization of the body of the Church, holy orders and matrimony.

In the *Eucharist* the paschal mystery, the mystery of Christ's death and resurrection, becomes present and the communion of the Church is expressed and accomplished. While Christ's actions at the Last Supper are repeated and his death on the cross is recalled, the sacrament is not just a historical commemoration but really makes present always and everywhere the death and resurrection of Christ.

Eucharist means thanksgiving. In celebrating this sacrament, the Church thanks God for his love expressed on the Cross and unites itself to Christ's prayer on the cross. All the sufferings of good people and the innocent are there, too.

Christ used the symbolism of this sacrament on the night of Holy Thursday. He took bread and, blessing it, declared it his Body, to be given up for men; then, taking the chalice with wine, he declared it his Blood, the blood of the new covenant. In this way he expressed the meaning of his death as a sacrifice of covenant and reparation for sins. Then he asked the apostles to repeat this action in his memory. Ever since, the Church has celebrated the Eucharist, making present anew, in all times and places, the death of Christ and the new covenant with God.

The priest imitates Christ's actions and repeats his words over the bread and the wine, consecrating them as the Body and Blood of Christ. And now that is what they really are. In eating the Body and drinking the Blood, we *participate in the sacrifice* and accept its fruits. The Church asks all the baptized to receive at least once a year, during the Easter time; but it is good for someone properly disposed to receive frequently, especially during the Sunday Eucharist, for this is how Christ's life within us is nourished.

As the union of each with Christ grows, the Church's unity also grows. The Eucharist expresses and at the same time builds up the Church.

But only those really united to that body can receive communion. That means only those who have been baptized, are members of the visible Church, and have not lost this spiritual union by sin. It should not be received by those not united to the Church or who believe they have committed a mortal sin.

In committing a grave or mortal sin, people lose the presence of the Holy Spirit in their souls and so lose their vital union with the mystical Body of Christ, the Church. They need to become live members again before receiving communion.

This can happen through another sacrament, the sacrament of *penance*, which also is called the sacrament of reconciliation or confession.

Since a Christian is part of a body, each of his or her sins and good actions has consequences for the whole body. Even a so-called private sin affects the whole Church, while everything good we do promotes its health.

In the sacrament of penance someone aware of having sinned approaches a priest who represents the Church and asks God's pardon. The priest extends pardon in the name of God and receives the person into communion with the mystical Body of Christ. The two things are inseparable, since union with God is through Christ's Body. This is why we should if possible seek God's pardon through the Church.

While one must approach this sacrament whenever he or she is aware of a grave offense against God, it is also good to ask pardon for ordinary sins and omissions, even though not grave. The Church asks those conscious of grave sins to go to confession at least once a year, when in danger of death, and when they wish to receive communion.

The Functions of the Body of the Church

As a body, the Church has various functions enabling it to fulfill its purpose of extending the mission of Christ in all ages and places and transmitting his doctrine and his life. Two sacraments organize the body of the Church: holy orders and matrimony. We turn to them now.

The sacrament of *holy orders* empowers some Christians to preach in Christ's name and provide the sacraments to others. While all Christians participate in the mission of Christ, and so have the duty of announcing his message, some are chosen and trained to announce the message publicly, in the Church's name. The sacrament of orders consecrates them for this work and guarantees them the help of the Holy Spirit. That assistance corresponds with their function in the Church: the highest authority in a diocese is its bishop, and for the Church at large the pope and the college of bishops in communion with him.

The sacrament of holy orders is administered by the bishop by imposing his hands upon the head of one being ordained. The person acquires power to preach the word of God in Christ's name and administer the sacraments.

Holy orders have, as it were, three degrees: bishop, priest, deacon. Each of them has different tasks: the deacon to preach, baptize, and officiate at weddings; the priest, besides this, to celebrate the Eucharist, forgive sins, and anoint the sick; and the bishop to do all this and to confer the sacraments of holy orders and confirmation (confirmation can be delegated to a priest).

The seventh on our list is the sacrament of *matrimony.* It sanctifies the natural institution of marriage and gives it a new, more profound meaning.

When a Christian woman and man receive each other as husband and wife, they create a bond that is not just a private relationship between the two of them or a juridical, social relationship, but also a special link to God and the Church—a union within another union, the Church. This is an open union, since the lives of children can be incorporated into it. Here is why each Christian family is called a domestic Church.

Matrimony is naturally ordered to the mutual communion of the spouses and to the founding of a family. It reinforces the union between spouses so that they will understand, respect, love, and help each other. It blesses their fertility: the children they bring into the world are not only theirs but also sons and daughters of God. And the sacrament gives them strength to educate their children and teach them to live as God's children.

St. Paul compares the union between spouses to the mystical union between Christ and the Church (see Ephesians 5:21–31). In marrying before God and the Church, people are joined in a special bond that gives them the grace to turn their marriages and families into real Christian communities where Christ's love holds sway.

Three of the sacraments are received only once—baptism, confirmation, and holy orders (once in each of its degrees). Two, anointing of the sick and matrimony, are received at special times and can be repeated. The other two, Eucharist and penance, can and should be received frequently because they nourish and sustain Christian life.

Catholicism

The Son of God became man and died on the cross to open for us the path that frees from sin and to enable us to become God's children. He spent the larger part of his life, some thirty years, engaged in the ordinary tasks of a man of his day. He seems to have been a carpenter (in the broad sense of that term). He worked with his hands and lived a normal life, thereby conferring upon even the most ordinary occupations and activities the ability to contribute to his own mission of redemption.

The years of his public life were spent explaining his doctrine, and gathering disciples and preparing them. After the shock of his seizure, condemnation, and death, a small group of these disciples—perhaps a hundred and fifty or so—persevered.

It was they whom Christ asked after his resurrection to continue his mission: "Go, therefore and make disciples of all nations, baptizing them in the name of the Father, and of the Son, and of the Holy Spirit, teaching them to observe all that I have commanded you" (Mt 28:18–19). He promised them the help of the Holy Spirit, who then came upon them at Pentecost. With this help, they immediately began to preach Christ's message courageously and incorporate new disciples into the Church. Since then—with great difficulties, advances, and setbacks—the Church has spread throughout the world.

The Church is universal by vocation. By the express desire of Christ, it is directed to all men and women, of all races, places, cultures, and times. "Catholic" is a Greek word meaning universal—open to all people and all worldly realities.

The whole man is involved, in all his dimensions: his work and rest, relationships with nature, other people, society, and God, all his ambitions and desires. There is more to being a Christian than now and then performing certain religious acts. Transformed into Christ, the Christian lives a life like his.

But to do that consistently one must have formation—one must become familiar with Jesus' life and doctrine. It also is necessary to receive the sacraments as sources of strength.

According to their abilities, all Christians have a duty to contribute to spreading Christ's message. But all things bear the stain of original sin and need to be renewed in Christ; all worldly realities need to be redeemed—culture, social structures, even nature. To achieve fulfillment, all things need Christ.

The method of salvation proposed by the Church in Christ's name begins in human hearts. It is in uniting human beings with God that the Church "solves" all the evils of the world—the internal disunity within each individual, the divisions among nations and peoples, even the disorder of the natural world. The Church's saving action is not directed to the organization of society or the shaping of culture or technical problem-solving. True, it may have implications in these areas, but fundamentally it is directed to the root of evil—sin, rejection of and separation from God.

The final fulfillment of everyone and everything is not possible in this world as we know it. Physical and, especially, moral limitations rule that out. Sin and the inclination to sin will remain embedded in human hearts until the end of time. This is true of Christians, and it affects the way they shape the Church down through history, concealing the truth of the Church by their sins.

Only at the end, when Jesus Christ returns to judge and purify everything, will the Church shine fully and be recognized by all as the place of God's salvation. Only then will Christ's mission be accomplished and sin completely vanquished. At best, the actions of Christians are for now a sign and a preparation for what definitive redemption will be.

But what will happen to those who know nothing about Jesus Christ and his Church? How can they come to know God, conquer sin, become God's children, be saved?

First of all, God wants us to make the effort to announce the gospel so that everyone can have the joy of meeting Christ and being joined to him in his Church.

Meanwhile, God operates in mysterious ways. We see only the surface of history. We cannot know how God acts in human hearts and, through them, in all human realities.

But we do know Christ has come for all. God abandons no one. He wants to save everybody and to incorporate all in the mystery of the death and resurrection of his Son. How he proceeds is not for us to know.

Those who don't know Christ or his Church may be really united to him. They, too, can receive God's Spirit if they are faithful to what conscience tells them God asks of them. It might be said that they belong to the Church's soul though not its body.

In this sense, too, the Church is catholic. As a sign of God's presence in the world and a sacrament of the world's salvation, it mysteriously gathers all people of all races, nations, and cultures, and in it all things human are renewed.

13

The Spirit of Christ

The Good News

If the Son of God had not lived among us, we would know nothing about God's inner life. "No one has ever seen God. The only Son, who is in the bosom of the Father, he has made him known" (Jn 1:18). By telling us he is God's true Son and speaking of the Holy Spirit, the Spirit of the Father and the Spirit of the Son, Christ has revealed what divine life is.

Human words express this mystery very poorly. Still, what they say is true: God's life consists of relationships of knowledge and love among the Father, the Son, and the Holy Spirit.

Christ is the Messiah, anointed by the Holy Spirit and true Son of God. The mystery of Christian morality lies in our being anointed with the Spirit and becoming God's sons and daughters through the mysteries of Christ's death and resurrection.This is the gospel, the good news Christ brought to the world. The sin of the world and death have been overcome by Christ, and in him we can vanquish sin and become children of God. The presence of the Holy Spirit in the soul makes us similar to Christ, in that it gives us a participation in his life.

Christian morality is thus the imitation and following of Christ. We are to learn from him as he is depicted in the gospels, imitate his actions, follow his counsels, meditate on his doctrine, attempt to share his sentiments. In every situation we must ask ourselves what our Lord would do, and then try to do it.

But Christian morality is not just an external imitation or following. It is a true repetition and assimilation of his life. Not a theory, not just a description of how to live, not simply the story of Christ's life, it is a true *participation in his life.* Christ then is the center of Christian morality.

The Holy Spirit's presence in the soul produces a real transformation by which Christ's spiritual features appear in the Christian. Faithful to the Spirit's promptings in our consciences, we are transformed little by little, without losing our identity. This does not come about simply by good actions and virtues, but by God's transforming action within us.

The saints, the men and women faithful to God, have very different personalities, but all resemble Jesus as he would have been had he lived in their circumstances. Indeed, by the action of the Holy Spirit, Christ in some way lives in them.

Through these men and women of God, the sanctifying power of the Holy Spirit is extended to the world. Wherever there is a just man or woman, the Holy Spirit is at work and God's salvation is taking place.

The effect of the transforming presence of the Holy Spirit in the soul is called *sanctifying grace*—"grace" because its presence is a marvelous gift from God, "sanctifying" because it makes us resemble Christ. It is a vital principle that enables us to live as God's children.

Next we shall consider some spiritual realities proper to Christians: the approach to God our Father, the Beatitudes, and charity.

Our Father

When Jesus' followers asked him how to pray, he told them to address God as Father: "Our Father who art in heaven, hallowed be thy name, thy kingdom come, thy will be done on earth as it is in heaven."

We have a right to do this because we are truly God's children, although Christ calls him Father from all eternity and we only from the time we received his Holy Spirit. St. Paul explains that we are children by adoption: "You have received the spirit of sonship. When we cry 'Abba! Father!' it is the Spirit himself bearing witness with our spirit that we are children of God, and if children, then heirs, heirs of God and fellow heirs with Christ, provided we suffer with him in order that we may also be glorified with him" (Rom 8:14–17).

In chapter 10 we saw that God deserves our full love. Now we see that the love we owe God is the love of sons and daughters. This deepens and enriches our understanding of the first commandment ("You will love the Lord your God with all your heart, and all your mind and all your strength") and also the other great commandment ("You will love your neighbor as yourself") inasmuch as the others are our brothers and sisters.

As children of God, we seek that his name be "hallowed," that is, that many people come to know him and love him. We care for what pertains to him. We ask for the coming of his kingdom—that the Kingdom of Christ may spread throughout the world and Christ's saving action reach everywhere.

We ask also that his will be done "on earth as it is in heaven." Christ said, "My food is to do the will of him who sent me," and this "food" also must be ours, which we discover in conscience, in the people and events around us, and in the teaching of the Church.

We should deal with God trustingly, asking him for things both material and spiritual: daily bread—our nourishment and release from all evils, help in physical and moral trials, and forgiveness of offenses "as we forgive those who trespass against us."

Knowing we are children of God gives a new meaning to our sins, since offending one's father is not the same as offending a stranger. The mystery of sin acquires new depth when we grasp sin's relationship to the Cross and see our sins as offenses against God.

But this same discovery removes that fear of divine vengeance for sin that followers of other religions may feel. Christians know God, our Father, does not take revenge. On the contrary, in the parable of the prodigal son Christ has left us a marvelous image of divine mercy.

Rather than taking revenge on the sinner, God from the Cross awaits his repentance. Having entered into the mystery of the Cross, which is the mystery of God's love, we should feel more strongly our duty to make reparation, while repentance should be much deeper than that of someone who only wants to avoid punishment.

Yet much less is enough for God. The prodigal son returns for no higher motive than knowing he would live better in his father's house, but that is enough for God to forgive him. So, in confession it is enough to repent because of fear of punishment or because of the ugliness of sin, though that will not satisfy one who knows what love is.Having spoken of God's fatherhood, we turn next to the motherhood of Mary.

Though not on the same level, the two things are mysteriously related. Christ as God is the true Son of God from all eternity, and as man, the true son of Mary. In identifying ourselves with Christ, we Christians are children of God and also children of Mary. As Christ loves his mother, so also he appreciates the affection Christians feel for her. That is the logic of love.

In Mary, too, we find the perfect realization of the salvific mission of Christ that makes her a model for all Christians. Preserved from sin from her conception and full of the grace of God and the gifts of the Holy Spirit, she is the first Christian: first to believe the mystery of Christ, first to place herself at the service of the mystery of redemption, and first to experience Christ's resurrection.

There is a great lesson in Mary's life. Though of all human beings the one most blessed by God who fulfilled his will most faithfully, she lived an outwardly ordinary life. She did nothing remarkable—except of course to love God with all her heart, mind, and strength, and love all people with God's love. Mary's message is that sharing in the salvific mission of Christ does not require great deeds. All human tasks will serve if done with love of God.

In the earliest days of the Church, before Pentecost, fearing to teach Christ's message, the first Christians gathered around Mary. Throughout history, she in whose womb Christ's physical body was formed has also been mother to the Body of Christ that is the Church. Thus, during the Second Vatican Council, Pope Paul VI solemnly declared her Mother of the Church.

The Features of Christ

Beginning in the fifth chapter of St. Matthew's Gospel and continuing through the seventh chapter, we find that remarkable discourse of the Lord called the Sermon on the Mount. Here Christ explains how those who want to follow him are to live.

The sermon begins with the beautiful passages setting out the Beatitudes. *Beatitude means happiness.* The Lord promises happiness to those who live as children of God. And he points to features they must have, which reflect Christ's way of acting and are repeated in each Christian, to say nothing of Mary and the saints."Blessed are the poor in spirit, for theirs is the kingdom of heaven. Blessed are those who mourn, for they shall be comforted. Blessed are the meek for they shall inherit the earth. Blessed are those who hunger and thirst for righteousness, for they shall be satisfied. Blessed are the merciful, for they shall obtain mercy. Blessed are the pure in heart, for they shall see God. Blessed are the peacemakers, for they shall be called sons of God. Blessed are those who are persecuted for righteousness' sake, for theirs is the kingdom of heaven. Blessed are you when men revile you and persecute you, and, utter all kinds of evil against you falsely on my account. Rejoice and be glad, for your reward is great in heaven" (Mt 5:3–12).

The items on this list all have a similar pattern. Jesus declares "blessed"—that is, happy—the members of some group or category of persons whom he then identifies; after that, he promises them a reward, phrased in various ways but in reality always the same.

The heavenly kingdom is the *kingdom of the children of God.* The world was created for them, and when it is purified from sin and justice is fully realized, it will be given to them. But our happiness will not come from possessing the world but from contemplating God.

The kingdom has come since Christ appeared in the world. He told his disciples it was within them. Wherever one finds a son or daughter of God ingrafted into Christ, there the kingdom is. The Church is, as it were, a sign of its presence and an anticipation of what will be at the end, when the kingdom is realized fully. Meanwhile, the kingdom expands insofar as God's children, transformed by grace, shape temporal realities as Christ would have them.

Let us now consider the several features praised by the Lord, which together form a spiritual portrait of the Christian.

The Lord praises the poor in spirit and the meek, those who weep, those who hunger and thirst for justice, the merciful and the pure of heart, those who work for peace, and those persecuted for their love of justice and their following of Jesus Christ. To resemble Christ, we must be like that: poor in spirit, suffering, enamored of justice, men and women of peace, and clean of heart. The Lord promises happiness to those who try to live like that—happiness at the end of time and also now.

Although it is not always possible to find an exact equivalent of the Lord's words, their meaning is clear enough.

To be *poor in spirit* means to be detached from earthly goods, not craving them, not devoting one's life to acquiring them, using them with sobriety, preferring simplicity. This is in contrast with the natural human tendency to hoard, in the belief that the more we have, the better. Ownership not only brings freedom (we can do more) but also restricts it, inasmuch as we become tied to things we own. To have a free heart—to love God above everything and one's neighbor as a child of God—one must be poor in spirit. "You cannot serve God and riches," says Christ a little later in the sermon (Mt 6:24).

To be poor in spirit also means being humble, not considering oneself superior to others. Humility does not dominate, does not presume, does not despise, is not vengeful. Its meaning is close to "meek" (one of those words that has no perfect translation), which refers to the sweetness proper to men and women of God. St. Bonaventure saw it reflected in the amiable, friendly, loving St. Francis of Assisi, and is a trait common to all saints. We see it also in our Lord—accessible to everyone, loving children, welcoming sinners, and forgiving those who wanted to harm him.

Blessed are they who mourn. And we might add: are without anger. Those who suffer the difficulties of life and unite themselves, consciously or unconsciously, to the sufferings of Christ on the Cross contribute by their pain to purifying their hearts and their behavior and also to purifying the world.

The Lord invites us to *hunger and thirst for justice*—to be upright, desiring that all be as they should. Lately, the idea of justice has come to be limited to economic relationships and the punishment of criminals. But its meaning in the Bible is much broader, where justice is almost the same thing as holiness. The just man loves God and seeks to do God's will. The just suffer at witnessing disrespect for God's law, mistreatment of a neighbor, disorderly attachments to earthly goods, the corrupting of sexuality, the social domination of private interests and selfishness, the abuse of the common good, the oppression of the weak, the suffering of the innocent.

The just are often persecuted for being just because their justice is a reproach to the unjust. Refusing to enter into shady deals or keep quiet about wrongful deeds makes them a bother to those who do such things.

The sin of the world and its remedy are visible in the persecution of the just. Here is why Christ suffered and suffers still. The just person is a sign of contradiction, revealing hearts—some because they become angry, others because they are moved and repent.

The *pure in heart* are upright men with the innocent hearts of children. Their purity of heart is opposed to the turbulence of the passions, to giving in to low desires, to disorders in eating and drinking. Especially it is opposed to lack of sexual control. Those who do not attain it in this life will have to purify their hearts in the next so as to love God above all things.

Since they have inner peace, men of God communicate peace. They work for peace and spread it. Sin divides people within themselves, separates them from God, and sets them in conflict with one another. Peace is a divine gift that comes with the eradication of sin. But the strength to vanquish sin comes always from God's grace, and so friendship with God is the foundation of peace.

The merciful are those sensitive to their neighbor's sufferings, with a greatness of heart that reflects God's own heart. As the love of God is merciful, so also a merciful Christian knows how to forgive. Spitefulness has no place in such a soul.

The blessedness of which the Lord speaks in the beatitudes is grounded in states or conditions that to merely human eyes look like misfortunes. Someone who supposes that human behavior is only an expression of primary instincts is adopting the morality of the animal kingdom. Survival and reproduction dominate here. Power and the satisfaction of appetites are the moving principles. Poverty, mercy, peace, justice, and a clean heart are meaningless.

But even natural morality goes beyond animal behavior by introducing a new element: intelligence. And Christian morality goes yet further, with a new element of its own: God's life.

The beatitudes reflect features of Christ that are naturally replicated in a Christian's conduct. These features come about through the Holy Spirit's transforming action in the soul. If they are found also in non-Christians, it is because God's Spirit also operates in them. This is the way of life of Christ, true God and true man.

With God's Love

Even though Christian morality isn't just a collection of principles and norms but the very life of Christ, Jesus at the Last Supper spoke of a commandment when giving his final instructions to his disciples: "This is my commandment, that you love one another as I have loved you. . . . This I command you, to love one another" (Jn 15:12, 17).

We saw that the Ten Commandments could be summed up as loving God above all things and one's neighbor as oneself. Christ's commandment contains something new. He does not ask us to love our neighbors as we love ourselves but to love them as he has loved them—with God's love.

We can do this because our identification with Christ is a participation in his life and therefore in his love—the love with which the Son loves the Father and God loves all men. St. Paul explains, "God's love has been poured forth into our hearts through the Holy Spirit which has been given to us" (Rom 5:5).

Divine love is very different from human love. Human beings tend to love what already is lovable. God's love is creative, making good—lovable—that which is loved. The world and what is in it exist because God loves them.

Love moves God to intervene in history and extends even as far as the Cross. Here, on the Cross, Christ shows how great God's love is, able to suffer injustice yet forgive the unjust and make them into God's children.

God wants his followers to be recognizable by this love of charity: "By this all men will know that you are my disciples, if you have love for one another" (Jn 13:35). Charity is a manifestation that one has received the Holy Spirit and new life in Christ.

This is how one becomes capable of following Christ, making him present in the world, suffering and forgiving. St. Paul sketches a profile of Christian charity in his first letter to the Corinthians: "Love is patient and kind; love is not jealous or boastful; it is not arrogant or rude. Love does not insist on its own way; it is not irritable or resentful; it does not rejoice at wrong, but rejoices in the right" (13:4–6).

This is not a calculating love. The Lord tells his disciples: "Love your enemies, and do good, and lend, expecting nothing in return . . . and you will be sons of the Most High, for he is kind to the ungrateful and the selfish. Be merciful, even as your Father is merciful" (Lk 6:35–36).

Charity like this is diametrically opposed to egoism, which is always on the outlook for what will benefit oneself. This doesn't mean one must be naïve, forever deceived and exploited. It means one must be Christ, constantly seeking the good of others, even at cost to oneself.

Like all loves, the love of charity has a certain order. It begins with those closest to us, but it must be open to all. It moves us to think of others before ourselves, to seek excuses before rushing to judgment, to forgive rather than seek vengeance, to suffer with everyone, understand everyone, help everyone. But in the end there is and can be no exhaustive list or catalogue, since the manifestations of charity are *the spontaneous fruits of the presence of the Holy Spirit in the soul.* Christ's morality arises from the prompting of charity, which are the impulses of the Holy Spirit in one's conscience, lived out in loving God and neighbor.

Thus, while Christian morality incorporates all valid principles of ethics and morals, it goes much further. Ethics seeks to organize human behavior by the order and measure of reason, but it cannot provide the inner strength to overcome sin and live by ethical norms. Christ's morality first heals the human person and supplies a new principle of action—the action of the Holy Spirit in the soul.

Charity is the distinctive characteristic of Christian morality. Saint's lives are marked precisely by that love, as is the history of the Church. True, one finds there abundant mediocrity as well. But this is true of all human affairs. The extraordinary fact is that men and women in all times and places have lived as children of God, making Christ present in their lives and loving as he did.

Earlier we saw that moral life begins when we start to overcome infantile selfishness. Now we see that the fullness of morality is a divine love that leads to self-giving without measure. St. Augustine speaks of two ways of life: "Two loves build up two cities: self-love to the point of despising God, the earthly one, love of God to the point of despising oneself, the heavenly one. That city seeks the glory of men, but this city has God as its highest aspiration, witnessed by one's conscience. . . . In the first one, the powerful and their minions are dominated by the desire of power; in the second, all serve each other in mutual love" (*City of God*, XIV, 28).

This is Christian morality, a morality not of negations but affirmations, not of limits but of fulfillment, not of slaves but of sons and daughters. Christian morality is the life of Christ as lived by ourselves. It might be called *the art of living in Christ.*

14

Bibliographical Note

I have not wanted to load the text with bibliographical references, but a few titles may be helpful to the reader who wants to go further. The literature of moral philosophy and moral theology is of course immense. Here I mention some works I would recommend to a friend.

The first point of reference is the doctrine of the Church. Blessed John Paul II deals with the foundations of Christian morality in his encyclical *Veritatis Splendor.* He also develops many moral themes in his social encyclicals, *Laborem Exercens, Sollicitudo Rei Socialis,* and *Centesimus Annus,* as well as documents such as his letter *Dilecti Amici* to the youth of the world (1985), which includes an excellent analysis of the use of freedom. Numerous interesting opinions can be found in the book-length interview by André Frossard, *Be Not Afraid.*

The third part of the *Catechism of the Catholic Church* is a basic reference point covering the core of Christian morality in simple language.

A number of authors present Christian morality in an attractive style—for example, C.S. Lewis in *The Abolition of Man, Four Loves,* and *The Problem of Pain*; G.K. Chesterton in his *Orthodoxy* and *The Everlasting Man*; E.F. Schumacher in *A Guide for the Perplexed* and *Small is Beautiful*; and Christopher Derrick in *The Delicate Creation.*

Among the classics, Plato's *Republic* and Aristotle's *Ethics* are of perennial importance. Seneca (*Moral Epistles to Lucilius*) and Cicero (*On Duties—De Oficiis*) deserve attention among Latin writers.

Two masterpieces stand out in the huge field of ancient Christian literature—*The Confessions* of St. Augustine and St. Thomas Aquinas's *Summa Theologiae*, parts I–II (human acts: the will, freedom, habits, and virtues); and II–II (the more important virtues, especially charity, prudence, justice, fortitude, and temperance). Walter Farrell's condensation *My Way of Life* can be helpful, as can *Elements of Christian Philosophy* by Etienne Gilson and Josef Pieper's *Fundamental Virtues.*

Pascal in his *Pensées* offers remarkable observations on human limitations and greatness. Dietrich von Hildebrand, a twentieth-century phenomenologist, is a good complement to the classical tradition: see his *Transformation in Christ* and *Ethics.* Other recent writers worth consulting include Robert Spaemann (*Basic Moral Concepts*), Jacques Maritain, Gabriel Marcel (*Being and Having*), Victor Frankl (*Man's Search for Meaning* and *Unconscious God*), Romano Guardini (excerpts in *The Essential Guardini*, edited by Heinz Kuehn), and Frank Sheed (*Theology and Sanity* and *Society and Sanity*).

The present volume owes much to St. Josemaría Escrivá. His books of aphorisms (*The Way*, *Furrow*, and *The Forge*) provide vivid, positive insights on the moral life, as do meditations such as "Respect for the Person and his Freedom," "Marriage a Christian Vocation," and "Interior Struggle" (in the book *Christ Is Passing By*).

Theologians of the Eastern churches worth consulting include Olivier Clément and Nicolas Cabasilas. The Russian novelist Fyodor Dostoyevsky has interesting ideas on sin, the Cross, and the communion of saints in books like *Crime and Punishment* and *The Brothers Karamazov.*

ADDENDA

Is Morality Relative?

Many of our contemporaries would answer yes without hesitation or thought. By "relative" they would mean "a matter of opinion," and they sincerely believe that morality is subject to individual tastes. Others would answer no—morality is immutable—meaning that moral precepts are the same for all people of all times. These positions obviously are not compatible. Some think morality is subjective, based on one's own tastes or decisions; others consider it to be objective, based on the reality of things.

The scholars of the Middle Ages held that, when there were conflicting opinions about a subject, it was necessary to distinguish so as to concede to each whatever truth it possessed. Indeed people do generally take their stand on truth of some sort. So let us proceed now in the same manner.

The Relativity of Mt. Everest

Considered in its own right, "relative" is a word of tremendous import, the exact opposite of "absolute." In the history of philosophy, the word absolute was a word reserved for God, or the divine, or the whole of reality. Thus, by comparison, everything else is always relative.

Among other things, the idea of the absolute implies that if we truly grasp its meaning, it can be thought of in only one way. This is part of the basis for the famous ontological argument for the existence of God of St. Anselm. On the other hand, everything that is not the absolute can be thought of in some other way: it can "not exist" or it can exist in some other form.

One can think of the world in many ways. J.R.R.Tolkien imagined a fantastic world with elves, orcs, and hobbits; it could have existed—nothing prevents this. And one can imagine other worlds, each with its own rules. There is no end to the number of worlds that can be imagined. Similarly, there could be an infinite number of moralities.

If we were made of a spongy material, it might be a gesture of esteem to whack elderly individuals with a club in order to stimulate their circulation and rejuvenate their tissues. The world and the human species could have been like that, but in fact they are not. Whacking old people with clubs would do them a lot of harm, so it is objectively cruel and unfair. Reality could be different, but it isn't.

This needs emphasizing inasmuch as it's central to nearly all of the confusions about morality. You can always imagine reality and morality being other than what they are. And in this sense, morality is relative.

Mt. Everest is relative in the same sense. It could be higher than it is (29,028 feet) or perhaps lower. Within some minimum of consistency, there is nothing that prevents it ending in three peaks or in eight, in pointed or in rounded peaks. Nothing prevents it from being a few miles further to the right or to the left of where it is. In this sense, it's relative. We can always imagine it being different.

Still, a pilot flying that way will be at pains to get the distances right. Yes, he can imagine Mt. Everest some other way, but it is where it is and he can't fly through it.

Someone acquainted with the third way to prove God's existence of St. Thomas Aquinas and Kantian morality might add interesting specifications. But they aren't necessary for the substance of the argument and are rather difficult, so we are not going to develop them now. For the moment it's enough to say that within a certain minimum degree of consistency, morality, like anything relative, can always be thought of in another way. To that extent we accept the view of those who hold that they can always imagine a different morality. Indeed they can. But as in the case of Mt. Everest, it's better to discover what exists.

The Threshold of Moral Experience

In a famous passage of the Nicomachean Ethics, Aristotle analyzes the motives of human actions. He identifies three: we can seek pleasure, or seek what is advantageous, or act because it is beautiful to act in that particular way. We can also act for the contrary reasons: to avoid pain or what is disadvantageous or what appears repugnant to us. Leaving aside exceptions, this way of classifying motives gives us a clue to moral experience.

Of course, many actions do have pleasure as their motive. We work because we enjoy working and seek to give ourselves pleasure. In other cases, we seek profit or advantage for ourselves. And we also do things because we feel we should do them (duties and obligations); it seems attractive to act in this way and unworthy to act in the other way (ideals of conduct). By these distinctions one judges what is moral.

There is a clear dividing line here. Action performed only for pleasure or advantage lies beyond the boundary of morality. The most important aspect is missing. This is why utilitarianism is inadequate as a program for a personal ethic. It can help in providing a minimal basis for political coexistence and, in some cases, for moral responsibilities. But the calculus of advantages does not make it possible to construct a system of morality that can serve to guide people. Rather it imprisons one in egoism. From this point of view, moralities based on tastes and aspirations are in reality not moral systems. Lacking moral resources, they can only be the camouflage or disguise of a pseudo-morality.

The existence of morality can be seen precisely in the existence of more motives than an egoistic calculation (personal or collective) of pleasures and interests. In admitting that some situations demand something of us beyond our pleasures and interests, we enter the sphere of morality—a way of acting that is beautiful and worthy of a human person and a way that is repugnant and unworthy.

Actually most people are intuitively aware that it is unworthy to place one's own pleasures and interests above everything. Normal persons of normal intelligence generally see such egoism as the essence of immorality, whereas sacrificing one's own pleasures and interests for the benefit of others—generosity and altruism, that is—are considered as the quintessence of nobility.

The first attitude is repugnant to ordinary moral sense, while the second arouses admiration. A fireman who risks his life to save a child, a captain who is the last to leave his ship before it sinks, parents who sacrifice their preferences to care for their children—all these are universally considered to be noble acts, models for imitation that elevate humanity and separate us from the law of the jungle. The consensus on these matters is practically universal and not based on rational argumentation.

Of course anyone can imagine some different foundation for morality—the desire to stand out from the crowd (one of the great intellectual passions) or egoism, a common passion that doesn't affect just intellectuals. There is no definitive argument to show that sacrifice is noble and egoism ignoble, and one can always deny that they are.

Let's go back to our first question: Is morality relative? I know an excellent business manager from whom I have learned some wise principles including this: "If you don't want to solve a problem, generalize it." The worst way to approach the question of whether morality is relative is to generalize. Instead let's look at morality as a whole and honestly consider what part of it might be relative.

Morality has three basic parts. One refers to relationships with others and is made up of duties of justice and solidarity. One refers to one's relationship with oneself and one's manner of life. And one refers to sexuality, marriage, and the family. Almost everything fits into one of these compartments. What part is relative?

The Most Universal Part of Morality: Justice and Solidarity

Since we are social beings and live in society, the broadest part of morality—a good 80–90% of it—refers to others and takes shape in duties of justice and solidarity.

Justice is based on equity—giving equally to those whose claims are equal, asking equally of those equally able to give. Since human beings are basically equal (in being human), all human relationships are based on a certain equity, a correspondence.

The most elemental part of equality concerns the respect others deserve. It is expressed in the so-called *golden rule* of morality, which is virtually universal: "Do not do unto another what you would not want for yourself." C.S. Lewis, in his beautiful book *The Abolition of Man,* offers an ample list of sources. It's very obvious, but, like everything, can be theoretically obscured or ignored.

A second area of justice concerns relationships between individuals. They are just when there is equilibrium and people do what they commit themselves to do. Here, too, there is spontaneous and universal agreement. To Cicero, this appeared to be the most elementary and obvious justice and the most necessary for civil order.

A third area concerns relationships between the individual and society or the human community. This is "distributive justice," according to which benefits and social tasks are distributed equitably—with a measure of equality—among members of a society. Equity, however, is not mere mathematical equality—it makes sense to pay more attention to those who need more and ask more from those who can give more. People who are governed require equity on the part of those who govern them. But one also can see the principle of equity at work in a process of "divvying-up" among children.

Finally, there are the duties of solidarity that express the inclination to help the needy members of society. This duty is always spontaneously recognized since it is natural for people with healthy instincts and values to feel compassion for their fellow men and put themselves in their place. Solidarity is linked to the common feeling of belonging. At times, therefore, it may extend only to those who are close; while slaves are excluded and strangers are hated.

How far must solidarity go? That is the basic thrust of the question in the gospel: "Who is my neighbor?" Jesus left no doubt: For a Christian, the neighbor is anyone he or she encounters. "Loving your neighbor as yourself" extends to all mankind because we are all children of God. This is also a fundamental assumption of the laws of democracies which take their ideals of equality and fraternity from the Christian cultural heritage. But even apart from Christianity, the same idea is found in many cultures which prescribe hospitality to strangers and foreigners.

In other cultures and at other times, one can observe limits placed on solidarity. We have mentioned slavery. War is another case: it is difficult to see that the enemy is a neighbor. There have been other historical instances. The Nazis pursued policies based on the inequality of peoples and races. The French revolutionaries known as Jacobins and the communists sacrificed the rights of people to the supposed interests of the state. These cases were not the products of different moralities, however, but of theoretical aberrations that repressed the common sense of morality. And even in the midst of horrors, through cracks in the theory, humanitarian sentiments could be seen, showing the human capacity to put oneself in the place of another. There are many beautiful examples that do honor to humanity.

The duties of justice and solidarity are almost universally recognized. They form the basis for recognition of human rights and, as we have said, of a very large part of morality. Thus, it is false to say that morality is relative, in the sense of being variable. Nearly everyone agrees on the greater part of moral principles and norms, while forcibly rejecting (with police and prisons) the claim that morality depends on personal tastes. Only some intellectuals oppose this view in theory, and some criminals in practice.

The Most Aristocratic Part of Morality: Self-dominion (Virtue)

In contrast to justice, the question of how to conduct oneself and live one's life is more complex. Moreover, it has a subjective component, since it depends on one's experience.

Young people tend to be sensitive to authenticity and to ideals, and they bring a great deal of idealism and radicalism to questions of justice. But they are less clear on the kind of life that they should live. Youthful views on entertainment and alcohol, for example, are not moral judgments but only indicate their visceral preferences. Young people are very passionate, easily swept away by strong or romantic emotions and lacking experience of life. They may feel sure that alcohol, speed, and fun are great, and they may call this a moral opinion. But it isn't such, because it's not based on a reasoned judgment about the reality of things, which they hardly know. Nor is it stable, because it will change with experience.

Young people do not see the impact on themselves, their families, and society that a disorderly life, devoted to drinking, passion, and partying can have. It doesn't trouble them to see a person drunk or under the influence of drugs—the sight is painful only to someone who has learned to love human dignity and conscience. Many years and much experience are needed to know what builds up and what destroys. So is personal experience of the goodness of sobriety.

When they mature, people know more and judge better about what makes for a good life. If they manage to live with rectitude, they will attain wisdom. A person is upright if he responds to what he believes is required and isn't turned aside by egoism or fear. Many, though not all, cultural traditions take such wise men and women as reference points. The central elements of human wisdom about life are universal. At bottom, they concentrate on asceticism: the ideal of self-control and sobriety. Beyond that, they concentrate on dedicating life to the great goods of contemplation of truth, art, and service to society. They discipline instincts in order to serve great goods. The great wise men of history—men such as Confucius, Buddha, Socrates, Plato, Aristotle, Seneca, St. Augustine, Gandhi—did not think other aspirations worthy of a human being. In the words of Max Scheler, "man is an ascetical animal." Only by renunciation can a person live at the level of his or her spirit.

Universal as this consensus is, though, it extends only to the wise, for not everyone is equally competent to judge in these matters. The more competent are those with a deeper and more accurate moral sense as the ancients knew very well. But they are not the only ones. We find the same insight in the conversation between Umberto Eco and Cardinal Martini: "The power of an ethic is judged by the behavior of the saints, not by that of the ignorant *cuius deus venter est* (whose god is their stomach)."

Personal morality is not democratic, and there is nothing strange about that. Science is not democratic either nor is art. Although we all have the same value as persons, we are not all equal as scholars, scientists, or writers. While each person's conscience must be respected, it makes no more sense to say that each person can shape a morality to suit his taste, than to say each can create his own science. We must learn from those with knowledge, grow in understanding by experience, and do our part to get things right, that is, to judge with rectitude in what refers to oneself without being misled by egoism or fear.

In this second area, the problem is not that morality is variable, but that our judgment and our moral quality vary. In life, as in a democracy, the need to respect everyone and not judge others' lives is one thing, but it is something very different to have to feign ignorance of the working of egoism, the importance of self-control, and the nobility of generosity, for these are virtually universal data of moral experience.

The Most Complex Area: Sexual Morality

Sexual morality is the area where the most problems arise. The claim that morality is relative is often a euphemism to justify sexual freedoms. Euphemisms conceal the harshness of reality and make life with others more pleasant, but they are obstacles to clear thinking, and are best revealed for what they are.

Sexual morality has some things in common with the other two areas of morality. For example, every sexual relationship with another person involves aspects of justice, sometimes very grave ones. To have a child generates very grave obligations and duties that go far beyond personal whim or preference. Repugnance is the universal human reaction to the egotist who puts his pleasures and interests above his duties toward others. To abandon wife and children on the excuse that one has fallen in love with someone else is a clear manifestation of egoism and a grave injustice. But it isn't hard to see why someone who acts this way should want to construct a new morality.

Sexuality also involves aspects of self-control related to the second area of morality. To let oneself be carried away by sexual infatuation is as unworthy and causes as much injustice and harm as becoming a slave to alcohol or drugs. Even more than other things, sexual pleasure requires asceticism because its pull is stronger. The virtually universal consensus of the wise is operative here as well, as in this saying of Epictetus: "As far as sexual pleasures are concerned, insofar as possible, one should preserve oneself pure before marriage and when united, share the legitimate pleasure" (*Enchiridion* 33,8).

Sexual pleasure and passion are often the most obvious aspects of sexuality, and they have their dignity and their purpose. But they are the less important aspects. Sexual morality requires that they be kept in their proper place.

From a biological point of view, sexuality serves reproduction. On the personal level, it serves conjugal love and interpersonal relationships. On the social level, it is linked directly to the common good, since it always concerns the future of society. These four dimensions (biology, conjugal love, family, and society) are the true framework of human sexuality and they are not abstractions but realities.

Although sexual morality can't be reduced to a few paragraphs, it is possible to sketch the framework. The first are the biological facts of sex. The male and female organs are complementary and there is a way of making use of sex that is natural and one might say, ecological; any other use is neither, though someone might want to argue otherwise. The natural and ecological order of sexuality is no more a matter of opinion than the working of the digestive system. To use sex without respecting its "given" character contradicts the biological reality of sexuality and to that extent is anti-natural and immoral.

Next comes what might be called the truth of human love. The love between a man and a woman is not love between bodies but between persons who mutually commit themselves. Other accounts of it have always been given by those who wish to justify the venting of sexual passion without the need for a personal relationship or a commitment. Many animals live this way, and human beings can imitate them. Nevertheless, there is a man-woman relationship in which sex expresses a commitment, a love that aspires to be eternal: this is conjugal love. It is founded upon a commitment of fidelity. Romantic failures themselves merely emphasize this, underlining the beauty and power of the ideal and also its difficulty.

The British singer Robbie Williams once said: "I have never been with a woman because I wanted to, but because I felt lonely. To be myself and dedicate myself to someone was unthinkable. I lacked the self-esteem necessary for that. I thought that if a woman fell in love with me, she was not worthwhile. When I stopped taking drugs five years ago and signed up with Alcoholics Anonymous, I promised myself I would get involved in a relationship only when I saw myself able to offer what a companion could hope for from me: sincerity and fidelity" (XL Semanal, 20, XI, 05, 26). He'd reached the point of wanting the ideal. What preceded it was something else. Let's hope that he has found it, although his point of departure was not very promising.

The third aspect of sexual morality is the family: the duties and joys of fatherhood and motherhood, and the life together of parents and children. It is a universal human experience that the most intense and enduring human relationships often arise here—and the tragedies that also arise when these don't go well simply indicate how deep the relationships can go, as well as the important duties of justice involved and the need to bend every effort to make things go smoothly.

The fourth aspect is social benefit. Unfortunately, the subject of the family is so artificially privatized today that truly "progressive" people regard it as bad taste to point out how much society's health and future depend on it. The family is an educational agent, a place of acceptance and social assistance, and an economic cell that motivates work, capitalizes saving, creates and stabilizes enterprises, and transmits professional experience. Elementary economic analysis makes it clear how much is at stake. The exigencies of social life may require tolerating mistakes and failures—while also seeking remedies for them—but it would be foolish not to recognize and protect the ideal.

Christian morality, a morality revealed by Christ, is founded directly on the ideal in all its aspects. It asks that marriage be permanent, that sex be used in a way that respects the natural biological order, that children be cared for until they are grown. Over the centuries, this has shed much light on marriage, providing a point of reference even for nonbelievers and resulting in many benefits that derive from this. Yes, conjugal love is demanding and often requires heroism. It's no game. It involves serious difficulties and, to turn out well, much time, dedication, and affection. This is the formula to make marriage work, while the more it's a story of I, me, and mine, the worse it turns out.

Sex can be considered a self-centered impulse carrying with it a right to personal pleasure, but it exists within the natural framework described here. Pretending differently is like imagining Mt. Everest in some other place.

Variations and Deformations of Morality

While morality, as we've seen, is in large part universal and has clear foundations, there have been different views on moral matters at different times. How one thinks of morality, depends on how one perceives reality. Each of us sees with his or her own eyes, and also judges as he or she has been taught.

So, for instance, the ideals associated with justice are clear enough, but racial hatred can obscure one's sense of equality.

Circumstances that make survival very difficult can give rise to very cruel social customs, especially in regard to the weakest (the sick, the elderly, slaves, prisoners). And just as there are egoistic and violent persons, so also there are societies with different degrees of egoism and violence that are transmitted to their members.

In any society, the requirement of survival, the need to preserve social order, and the experience of life tend to require criteria of justice, personal moderation, and rather rigid sexual discipline. No society could survive in which there was a general lack of sexual discipline. Children are a good of the first order for parents and for society, and this is why all stable societies insist on the observance of strict sexual laws (though of course there are some variations and violations). Since the goods at stake are very real, so are the rules.

Our society has attained very high levels of moral sensitivity in regard to justice and solidarity. This sector of morality has never been so clear and so respected. Despite some sad inconsistencies to be mentioned later, this is a great accomplishment that deserves to be cherished.

In matters of life style, however, ours is a consumer society, dominated by advertising whose pressure is as ubiquitous as the air we breathe, and directly opposed to the ideals of a life of sobriety. Society admires such ideals when it encounters them in monks and nuns, missionaries and volunteers, but it hardly needs saying that it does not imitate them. And so this society is unable to educate its young people. No one dares to ask them for sacrifices, even though placing duty before appetite is the most elementary training for the moral life. Rather, we envy youth their ability to indulge themselves without obligations. We have become a society of Peter Pans—childish individuals who refuse to grow up.

The biggest changes have been in regard to sexual morality. They amount to an unprecedented revolution, reflecting not moral progress, but simply the expansion of technical means for separating sexual pleasure from its natural consequences, thus also robbing sexual relations of their natural meaning and seriousness of purpose. The result is a generalized "sexualization" to which pornography testifies, along with a trivialization of sexual behavior. After the fact, attempts have been made to develop new moralities to rationalize what has happened, but these efforts are not persuasive.

Actually, the natural and moral framework of sexuality has not changed. Its four aspects are the same, and personal happiness and the future of society continue to be linked at the deepest level to the family. Reality is as it is. Promiscuity and alternative families have been tried, with disastrous results, by the totalitarian systems of the twentieth century. And it should be obvious that a society made up of dirty, old, unmarried men has no future.

Sexual pressure has destabilized the family bond and obscured the duties of justice that pertain to children and spouses. Radical political parties continue to promote divorce. They place the rights and sexual whims of the individual above the family bond, the rights of the other spouse, the rights of children and the permanence of the home (a crucial right, considering the damage done when it is violated). But this is not some new morality in which new moral principles have come to light. All that has happened is that sexual egoism has made a violent attack on other values that are more important but more vulnerable.

One result is a grave obscuring of the value of life. Contraceptive devices facilitate promiscuity, but they sometimes fail (or their users do). So we have unwanted children begotten in abnormal circumstances. The subsequent pressure to get rid of them has helped produce one of the saddest changes yet in the public sense of morality. While a child who has been born is a citizen protected by law, the unborn child is denied protection. Abortion is legal in many places, and disposing of a child is hardly more of a medical issue than getting rid of a wart.

In a cultural setting like this, the argument that everyone is entitled to his or her own view of morality is purely an exercise in euphemism. There is no great moral debate, and such passion as we see is the passionate desire to prevail. People do as they please, and the result isn't a new morality but no morality. No one abandons his wife, has an abortion or is sexually promiscuous on the basis of a new morality. Rather they have either lost or simply never had a moral view of sexuality. Often it's not their fault. No one has taught them anything else. The society that has trivialized sex has nothing to say to a young woman alone with a problem except to tell her to take the easiest, but saddest, way out.

Conclusion

It's a hypocritical temptation to shape morality according to what people happen to do. "When the heart gives itself up to the pleasure which seduces it, reason abandons itself to the error which justifies it." So says Cicero (*On the nature of the Gods*, I, 54). Deeds should be shaped by morality—and *not* a morality devoted to defending egoism. The acid test of any morality is precisely the sacrifice of personal interest on the altar of higher value. Immorality is essentially the reverse.

If our culture's worst distortion of values is in relation to sexual morality, the second worst concerns life ideals. Moral sensitivity today stresses questions of justice while conventional wisdom holds that in the private sphere everyone has a right to his or her own morality. But in reality there aren't different moralities, just different ways of behaving.

Social life requires respect for others and tolerance of their opinions. The private sphere of life must also be respected, provided it does not damage the common good. But it does not follow that anything and everything can be moral. Ideas do indeed have consequences, and not all ideas and consequences are good.

Much has been said here about what morality is and what it is not stands in need of development. How moral convictions are formed, how they become present in conscience, and how they are shared and transmitted in a society are matters of great importance. Here we have only sketched some basic outlines.

It's a bad habit, intellectually speaking, to seize upon the obscure points of a position in order to cast doubt on the whole of it. This often happens with morality. If one point is questionable, then all of morality must be relative, a matter of opinion. But this is like declaring the pyramid of Cheops unreal because it's not exactly a pyramid. Morality, with its three levels of justice, personal asceticism, and the natural framework of sexuality, is not a product of the imagination depending on each individual's whims. Although not so visible as the pyramid of Cheops or Mt. Everest, it's nevertheless much more real than either, with a far greater impact on people's happiness and the future of society.

This is not a matter of religious faith. It's as accessible to someone without the gift of faith as to someone who has that gift. Still, faith does add assurance, confirming that at the heart of reality lies an intelligible order willed by God. This was beautifully expressed in the first century a.d. by the wise Jew, Philo of Alexandria. Commenting on the first book of the Bible, Genesis, which for pious Jews forms part of the Law (the Torah), he said: "This beginning is more wonderful than one could say, because it includes the narration of the creation of the world in which is implicit that the world is in harmony with the Law and the Law with the world and that the man who respects the Law, in virtue of that respect, becomes a citizen of the world by the simple fact that he conforms his actions with the will of nature by which the entire universe is governed" (*De Op. Mundi*, I, 1–3).

Note: This is a translation of an article by the author in the January 2006 issue of *Nuestro Tiempo.*

INDEX

D

E

F

H

I

J

K

L

M

N

O

P

U

V

W